To Priscilla
with gratitude and admiration

Vanishing Circles
Portraits of Disappearing Wildlife
of the Sonoran Desert Region

BY LINDA M. BREWER

FOREWORD BY
RICHARD LEAKEY

ESSAYS BY MICHAEL BALDWIN AND RICHARD C. BRUSCA

THE ARIZONA-SONORA DESERT MUSEUM PRESS

© 2010 Arizona-Sonora Desert Museum

All rights reserved. All texts copyright © by Arizona-Sonora Desert Museum. All art images reproduced courtesy of the artists and protected by copyright © by each respective artist.

Published in the United States of America by
Arizona-Sonora Desert Museum Press
2021 N. Kinney Road | Tucson, Arizona 85743
520-883-3028 | asdmpress@desertmuseum.org
www.desertmuseum.org

ISBN 978-1-8866-79-41-2

Copyright registered with the U.S. Library of Congress

The Vanishing Circles exhibition and publication were funded by grants from the Priscilla and Michael Baldwin Foundation.

Book development and editing by Richard C. Brusca, Director, Arizona-Sonora Desert Museum Press

Design by Bailwick, Ink

Printed in Canada by Friesens

Front cover: Algodones Dunes, by William Hook
Back cover: ocelot, by Edward Aldrich
Pages 136-39: fishes and frog, by Rachel Ivanyi
All illustrations within narratives by Kim Duffek

CONTENTS

Acknowledgments	iv
Foreword RICHARD LEAKEY	v
Conservation through Art Education MICHAEL BALDWIN	1
Artwork Contents by Subject	2
Map of the Sonoran Desert Region	4
The Portraits	5
Conservation Work at the Arizona-Sonora Desert Museum RICHARD C. BRUSCA	136
The Vanishing Circles Collection MICHAEL BALDWIN	138
The Artists	140
Artwork Contents by Artist	150
Suggested Readings and References	152
Common and Scientific Names for Species in Narratives	154
Agencies Designating Species Conservation Status	156
Glossary	158
Index	162
Author's Acknowledgments	166

The Desert Museum will be forever grateful to Priscilla Baldwin for her passion and profound vision in establishing the Arizona-Sonora Desert Museum's Art Institute and the Vanishing Circles project, and to the Priscilla and Michael Baldwin Foundation for its support of conservation and art at the Museum. Special thanks go to the Luce Family Fund for their generous contribution of two paintings in the Vanishing Circles collection. The success of the exhibition and this associated book benefited enormously from the expertise of Susan Fisher. Linda Brewer's exceptional talents made the book a reality; she is not only an accomplished writer but also a gifted natural historian and graphic designer of the first order. The many artists who have participated in the Vanishing Circles project have done so with a sense of joy and commitment, and it is their fine work that will engage people and inspire them to care for the natural world.

Craig S. Ivanyi, Executive Director
Robert J. Edison, Executive Philanthropy Director
Richard C. Brusca, Senior Director, Science and Conservation

Foreword

Overpopulation, habitat destruction, pollution, overfishing of the world's oceans, the introduction of invasive species, global warming, and countless other human-driven assaults to nature are rapidly degrading our unique planet. Never has the importance of public awareness of conservation been more important, as species are daily driven to extinction—most before they have even been named or described. In the Sonoran Desert alone, over two-dozen species or subspecies of wildlife have gone extinct through the actions of humans. This is not a new problem. Across the world, the rate of species loss as a consequence of human actions has accelerated. We know of the iconic species such as tigers and elephants, but these represent a tiny fraction of what we are losing daily. Good science and education are crucial to the efforts being made to stem the catastrophe that is unfolding.

With its long history of research and education programs, there is no better institution than the Arizona-Sonora Desert Museum to rise to this occasion in the unique landscape of the Sonoran Desert. The Desert Museum excels in many ways, but perhaps the most important is its deep commitment to conservation. They don't just talk about it, or trifle with it; they execute it—with scientific rigor and breadth of action. This world-class institution has played pivotal roles in a number of far-reaching conservation initiatives, including the establishment of protected island sanctuaries and coastal wetlands in the Gulf of California, the establishment of a tropical deciduous forest reserve in Sonora, designation of the Ironwood Forest National Monument in southern Arizona, development of the award-winning Sonoran Desert Conservation Plan in Pima County, Arizona, and many others.

The Desert Museum's Vanishing Circles art collection (and exhibition) is not only delightful and edifying in and of itself, it is also a creative and effective tool for promoting conservation. Art, like nature, is an inspiration, and bringing these unique and rare species into the public eye through paintings, drawings, and highlights of their life stories will engage and inspire thoughtful people to consider their own actions, both positive and negative, and how those actions ripple into the wild world. It should inspire them to care about biodiversity on Earth and in the Sonoran Desert in particular. This informative and artistic book brings a novel and dynamic view of the region's vulnerable, threatened, and endangered species and landscapes to readers everywhere.

We must care about these species. Species are inextricably linked to each other and to us in both subtle and obvious ways. If we don't learn to save species, we will never save ecosystems, and it is the natural ecosystems of the Earth that humans depend on for their own well-being and sustenance.

Richard Leakey, FRS
Professor of Anthropology
Stony Brook University

For information about scheduling the Vanishing Circles exhibition at your institution, please contact the Art Institute of the Arizona-Sonora Desert Museum at (520) 883-3024 or write *arts@desertmuseum.org*.

Conservation Through Art Education

Michael Baldwin
Trustee, Arizona-Sonora Desert Museum

"*L*ook at your fish" — Louis Agassiz, 1847, at the Lawrence Scientific School, Harvard University.

> *In ten minutes I had seen all that could be seen in that fish….Half an hour passed—an hour—another hour; the fish began to look loathsome. I turned it over and around; looked it in the face—ghastly; from behind, beneath, above, sideways, at three-quarters view—just as ghastly. I was in despair.*
>
> *I might not use a magnifying glass; instruments of all kinds were interdicted. My two hands, my two eyes, and the fish: it seemed a most limited field. I pushed my finger down its throat to feel how sharp the teeth were. I began to count the scales in the different rows, until I was convinced that was nonsense. At last a happy thought struck me—I would draw the fish, and now with surprise I began to discover new features in the creature.*"

At this point professor Agassiz told his student to look again.

> *I was piqued; I was mortified. Still more of that wretched fish! But now I set myself to my task with a will, and discovered one new thing after another.*
>
> *The afternoon passed quickly; and when, towards its close, the professor inquired: "Do you see it yet?"*
>
> *"No," I replied, "I am certain that I do not, but I see how little I saw before."**

Samuel Scudder, student
As described in *Brave Companions* by David McCullough (NYC: Simon & Schuster, 1992)

Samuel Scudder went on to become a respected entomologist. Can there be any doubt that he remembered his "loathsome" fish with affection throughout his life?

This example demonstrates perfectly the primary concepts and methods of the Arizona-Sonora Desert Museum Art Institute. "Conservation through Art Education" is the mission statement and notion promulgated by the Art Institute and its founder, Priscilla Baldwin. Students at the Art Institute scrutinize specimens of many species in great detail, producing paintings and drawings that accurately and artistically portray the flora, fauna, and environments of the Sonoran Desert Region. Intense study of this sort instills a deeper understanding and a love and concern for the natural history of the region. As more students pass through the programs at the Art Institute, the ranks of naturalists and conservationists will increase in like measure and become a powerful influence in the preservation of species and habitats.

With the Vanishing Circles exhibition and its companion publication, the Arizona-Sonora Desert Museum draws attention to a wide variety of flora, fauna, and habitats found in this vast region, and to the extreme fragility of the various ecosystems. The artists represented in this exhibition have used paint or graphite, scratchboard or pen, to focus attention on a region at risk and encourage conservation awareness.

How would we explain to future generations why we allowed these ecosystems to deteriorate without making an effort to conserve them? No explanation would suffice.

Artworks by Subject

		PAGE	ARTIST
Amphibians and Reptiles	American Crocodile	7	Rachel Ivanyi
	Desert Tortoise	9	Carel P. Brest van Kempen
	Desert Tortoise	11	John N. Agnew
	Giant Spotted Whiptail	13	Carel P. Brest van Kempen
	Gila Monster	15	John N. Agnew
	Mexican Beaded Lizard	17	Carel P. Brest van Kempen
	Ramsey Canyon Leopard Frog	19	John N. Agnew
	San Esteban Chuckwalla	21	Carel P. Brest van Kempen
	Sea Turtles	23	Rachel Ivanyi
	Sonoran Tiger Salamander	25	Michael James Riddet
	Tarahumara Frog	27	Rachel Ivanyi
	True Frogs	29	Rachel Ivanyi
Fishes	Apache Trout and Gila Trout	31	Rachel Ivanyi
	Desert Pupfish and Quitobaquito Pupfish	33	Rachel Ivanyi
	Fishes of the Colorado River	35	Rachel Ivanyi
	Fishes of the Gila River	37	Rachel Ivanyi
	Fishes of the Río Yaqui	39	Rachel Ivanyi
Invertebrates	Huachuca Giant Skipper	41	Michael James Riddet
	Aquatic Invertebrates	43	Scott Fraser
Birds	Abert's Towhee	45	Joe Garcia
	Bald Eagle	47	Edward Aldrich
	Cactus Ferruginous Pygmy Owl	49	Rachel Ivanyi
	California Brown Pelican	50	Janet Heaton
	California Brown Pelican	51	Edward Aldrich
	California Condor	53	Carel P. Brest van Kempen
	Least Bell's Vireo	55	Michael James Riddet
	Masked Bobwhite	57	Joe Garcia
	Northern Aplomado Falcon	59	Larry Fanning
	Osprey	61	Edward Aldrich
	Rufous-winged Sparrow	63	Michael James Riddet
	Thick-billed Parrot	65	Edward Aldrich
	Violet-crowned Hummingbird	67	Adele Earnshaw
	Western Burrowing Owl	68	Anne Peyton
	Western Burrowing Owl	69	Richard Sloan
	Western Yellow-billed Cuckoo	71	Michael James Riddet

	PAGE	ARTIST	
Black-footed Ferret	73	Nicholas Wilson	Mammals
Black-tailed Prairie Dog	75	Priscilla Baldwin	
Jaguar	77	John Seerey-Lester	
Margay	79	Martiena Richter	
Merriam's Mouse	81	Michael James Riddet	
Mexican Gray Wolf	83	Larry Fanning	
Mt. Graham Red Squirrel	85	Nicholas Wilson	
Ocelot	87	Edward Aldrich	
Pronghorn	89	Nicholas Wilson	
Spotted Bat	91	Carel P. Brest van Kempen	
Arizona Claret Cup Cactus	93	Constance Sayas	Plants
Bristol's Hedgehog Cactus	95	Bobbie Brown	
Desert Ironwood Tree	97	William Hook	
Desert Night-blooming Cereus	99	Rhonda Nass	
Kearny Sumac	101	Dulce Nascimento	
Kearny's Bluestar	103	Manabu C. Saito	
Nichol's Turk's Head Cactus	105	Livia Vieira	
Organ Pipe Cactus	107	William Hook	
Pima Pineapple Cactus	109	Joan McGann	
Pima Pineapple Cactus Flower	110	Rhonda Nass	
Pima Pineapple Cactus Fruit	111	Rhonda Nass	
Sabo's Pincushion Cactus	113	Bobbie Brown	
Slender Climbing Cactus	115	Rhonda Nass	
Altar Valley	117	John N. Agnew	Habitats
Aravaipa Canyon	119	Ken Stockton	
Gran Desierto de Altar/Algodone Dunes	121	William Hook	
Sabino Canyon	123	Ken Stockton	
San Pedro River	125	Less Lull	
San Pedro River	127	Shari Jones	
Sea of Cortez, Mangrove Bay	129	William Hook	
Sea of Cortez	131	William Hook	
Tropical Deciduous Forest	133	Ken Stockton	
Vanishing Species	135		

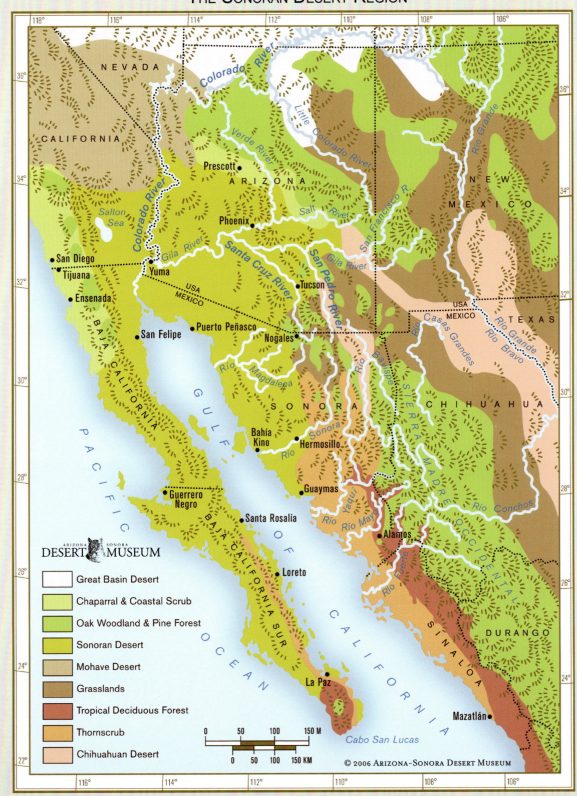

The Portraits

The 67 works of art in the Vanishing Circles exhibition portray 93 vulnerable, endangered, or extirpated species indigenous to the Sonoran Desert Region (which includes the Gulf of California) and 7 landscapes that offer vital habitat for these and myriad other species. Although the exhibit could not be all-inclusive for obvious reasons, the artworks selected illustrate a range of species and classes in the animal and plant kingdoms that are literally losing ground—or water, as the case may be. (The Vanishing Circles project is also ongoing, and more threatened species and habitats are being portrayed for future exhibitions.) The conservation status given for the species on these pages may change over time, but up-to-date information can be accessed online at websites for organizations or agencies designating species conservation status, addresses for which are included at the back of this book.

The landscapes and the amphibian, reptile, fish, bird, mammal, plant, and invertebrate portraits artfully rendered on these pages present a plea for all the species and habitats at risk in the Sonoran Desert Region. Impacts of our growing human population—including habitat loss and degradation, the introduction of nonnative species, and climate change—continue to increase environmental pressures, bringing these creatures and habitats ever closer to extinction. It is easy to imagine that the loss of little-known or noncharismatic species might not be critical, but each species, no matter how lowly, plays a unique and in no way insignificant role in its local circle of life. As more threads are broken, our ecosystems are compromised and nature's ability to recover is diminished, jeopardizing not only our natural habitats but also the health and well-being of our children, and their children. In light of this, the Arizona-Sonora Desert Museum, its supporters, and partners are working to stay the loss of species. As you turn the pages of this book, we welcome you to join us.

AMERICAN CROCODILE
Crocodylus acutus

Crocodiles, you may be surprised to learn, are more closely related to birds than to most other reptiles. Birds and crocodiles are the only extant members of the Archosauria, an ancient group descended from the dinosaurs. Like many of nature's ancient survivors, crocodiles evolved with some curious but persistently useful characteristics. Their socketed teeth are lost and replaced repeatedly throughout their life; although they have less than two dozen teeth in their long snouts, an adult crocodile can have *thousands* of teeth over a lifetime. (You can tell the difference between alligators and crocodiles, which belong to entirely different families though both are loosely referred to as "crocodilians," by looking at their teeth. Unlike alligators, crocodiles have a large fourth tooth near the front of the lower jaw that stays outside the upper lip when the jaw is closed, and with jaws closed a crocodile's teeth are more visible in general. The tip of an alligator's snout is more rounded than a crocodile's. Also, alligators are most often found in freshwater habitats, while crocodiles tend to saltwater habitats.) Crocodiles possess the most powerful jaws of the animal kingdom, with a biting strength several times greater than sharks or hyenas. But they are gentle with their own young, guarding their eggs and carrying young hatchlings to water. They are the only reptiles with a four-chambered heart.

Another attribute that distinguishes crocodiles from most other reptiles is their ability to run in a "high walk" with legs nearly beneath them, though they also ambulate in a "belly walk" with legs splayed out, a posture more typical of reptiles. They are strong swimmers and spend long hours immersed in water, with just the eyes, ears, and nostrils above the surface as they wait to snap up prey. Fish constitute the bulk of their diet, but birds, mammals, and many aquatic or amphibious animals fill out the menu. The American crocodile is a large species, 15 to 20 feet in length at maturity, and it enjoys the rank of top predator with few natural threats. Unfortunately, threats from human society are dire.

Crocodilians survived the mass extinction that put an end to the dinosaurs, but extant crocodile species around the globe are in steady decline, and the American crocodile is already threatened with extinction. On the East Coast, American crocodiles are found from Florida to Venezuela. On the West Coast, this species used to occur as far north as the coast of Sonora, Mexico. Now, American crocodiles range from the lower end of the Sea of Cortez, along the coast of Sinaloa, Mexico, south to northern Peru. This Pacific population is especially endangered. Like other crocodile species, they inhabit coastal wetlands, nesting in shallow, brackish habitats and estuaries near mangroves. In recent decades, development along the coast has destroyed much of their habitat, including important nesting areas. In addition the crocodile has been killed for its leather, for food, and even for illegal sport. In 1975, it was listed as endangered in the United States, and Mexico later barred the hunting of all crocodiles. Fortunately, most countries where American crocodile are found signed the CITES agreement prohibiting its international trade, significantly reducing the taking of crocodiles for their hide. In the United States, it was downlisted from endangered to threatened in 2007.

AMERICAN CROCODILE
watercolor, 15" x 20"

RACHEL IVANYI

IN THE LAST FEW DECADES, THE POPULATION OF
MOJAVE DESERT TORTOISES HAS
DROPPED ALMOST 90%.

DESERT TORTOISE
Gopherus agassizii

La tortuga. The sounds bump and roll out of the mouth, solid like the thing itself. Tortoise. Desert tortoises are dense and squat, domed, hard-plated shells on stout legs, with a long neck and short tail—an iconic shape found in ancient art of the Southwest. Slow-moving and long-lived (up to 40 years or more), these armored herbivores have a visual acuity and strong sense of smell that direct their wanderings in a variety of landscapes—from washes and flatlands in the Mohave and Colorado Deserts, to rocky hillsides or sandy soils in the Sonoran Desert, to thornscrub and tropical deciduous forest in Sonora, Mexico. Though toothless, tortoises have a birdlike beak and strong tongues with which they bite off desert grasses and wildflowers, or cactus pads and fruits in the summer. Well adapted to arid lands, they can get nearly all their moisture from the food they eat, surviving almost entirely without drinking water. A specialized urinary system allows them to isolate and retain large quantities of water in their bladder.

There are two populations of desert tortoise in the American Southwest (and another in Sinaloa, Mexico), each with distinct behavioral and morphological differences. (All of these populations have also been found to be genetically distinct and may be named separate species in the future.) The Mojave Desert tortoises, in northwestern Arizona and adjacent states, dig burrows up to 35 feet long. These burrows harbor a number of tortoises for winter hibernation. Over the last few decades, the Mojave Desert tortoises have suffered from an infectious disease of the upper respiratory tract and a disease that degrades their shells, as well as from degradation of their habitat by livestock, mining, and all-terrain vehicles (ATVs). These assaults, and extensive predation of hatchlings by ravens, have precipitated almost a 90% drop in their population.

continued

DESERT TORTOISE
acrylic, 21" x 30"

CAREL P. BREST VAN KEMPEN

> DESERT TORTOISES GROW—VERY SLOWLY—FROM ABOUT 2 INCHES AT HATCHING TO 14 INCHES OR SO AT FULL MATURITY.

DESERT TORTOISE *continued*

Tortoises of the Sonoran Desert tend to be solitary, except when breeding. But even when male-female contact is restricted by drought or declining populations, females can produce fertile eggs using sperm held in their cloaca for two years or more. Desert tortoises reach sexual maturity when their shell is about seven inches long (between 13 and 15 years of age). They grow, very slowly, from 2 inches or so at hatching to 14 inches or so at full maturity. Gila monsters, coyotes, and roadrunners, among others, prey on tortoise eggs and young.

To date, the Sonoran population, though probably in decline, is not critically threatened like the Mojave population. In times of drought, tortoises tend to stick to their burrows, and low counts in recent years may be due in part to their limited presence above ground during the current long-term drought. Even so, the incursion of roads, residential and agricultural development, and off-road vehicles into their habitat is a serious concern, as is the spread of nonnative grasses that bring wildfire to desert creatures not at all adapted to fire. In addition, well-intentioned efforts to mitigate habitat loss have shown that these tortoises have a low rate of survival after relocation. Desert tortoises are protected by law from collection and vandalism. Unfortunately, the indirect assaults have been little addressed.

DESERT TORTOISE
scratchboard, 8" x 11"

JOHN N. AGNEW

Giant Spotted Whiptail
Aspidoscelis burti stictogrammus

This impressive lizard spends its days aggressively hunting spiders, beetles, scorpions, and other arthropods, poking brashly through leaf and grass litter, head swaying left and right. On occasion, it will also eat small lizards or other small vertebrates. A subspecies of the canyon whiptail (*Aspidoscelis burti*) in the family Teiidae, the giant spotted whiptail is larger than any of the other subspecies, with adults measuring 11 to 18 inches nose to tail tip. Compared to the slim-bodied look of other whiptails, they are fairly stocky. Young lizards are striped lengthways, but on mature lizards those stripes will have changed to blue-gray or greenish spots, while a reddish hue appears on the head and neck. Although the crackle of foraging through dry vegetation makes them conspicuous, giant spotted whiptails are exceptionally leery and quick to retreat from onlookers; even so, many fall prey to snakes, roadrunners, and raptors.

Biologists have been particularly interested in the genus *Aspidoscelis*, perhaps because about one third of the whiptail species in the southwestern United States and northern Mexico reproduce asexually, with females laying eggs that are clones of themselves; but *A. burti stictogrammus* is not one of them. Twenty-odd members of this genus range across most of the United States and Mexico, and south as far as Costa Rica. All lay eggs, and share certain physical features, such as pointed heads, forked tongues, boxy scales on the underside, and very long tails. Like other ectotherms, which regulate body temperature by the heat of the sun (or sun-warmed air, rock, or ground), giant spotted whiptails are primarily diurnal. In winter they simply avoid the coldest months, remaining dormant until temperatures rise to an optimum level, usually in April or May.

Giant spotted whiptails make their homes in grassy patches and in densely vegetated areas in desert scrub, in cottonwood and sycamore-dominated riparian corridors, woodlands, tablelands, washes, and canyons in the Sonoran Desert Region. They are found in southeastern Arizona (including the Santa Catalina, Santa Rita, Baboquivari, and Parjarito Mountains), far southwestern New Mexico, and northern Sonora, Mexico. Although this species is not listed as threatened or endangered in the United States, its small population and limited range give it special status as a sensitive species with the Bureau of Land Management and the U.S. Forest Service, which manages much of its habitat in the United States. The New Mexico Department of Game and Fish lists it as a threatened species. Habitat loss is the greatest threat to this reptile.

Although this species is not listed as threatened or endangered in the United States, its small population and limited range make it vulnerable to natural or anthropogenic threats. Habitat loss is the greatest threat to this reptile.

Carel P. Brest van Kempen
Giant Spotted Whiptail
acrylic, 30" x 20"

Gila Monster
Heloderma suspectum

Given the creature's striking black-and-orange, -coral-, or -pink-patterned beads, overstuffed shape, and venomous reputation, it isn't surprising that Gila monsters have inspired fear and awe. At close to 2 feet in length, they are the largest lizards native to the United States. These improbable creatures deliver venom with almost every bite of their powerful jaws. They may not have an option. The predominant theory is that the toxin is automatically released through a groove in their teeth when the jaws clamp hard into flesh or other substance, although a few instances of apparently "dry bites" have been reported in recent years. This envenomed bite brings agonizing pain to animals, and a Gila monster will often fix itself on the unfortunate recipient for an extended time.

Contrary to common belief, these venomous lizards are not only nocturnal; they are active throughout the day. They are seldom seen because they simply spend little time outside, venturing out of their burrows only for brief hunting forays. In winter, however, Gila monsters can sometimes be seen basking in the sun after stirring from a late-fall through early-winter hibernation. In the fall, they lay eggs in the burrow from which the hatchling will emerge in the early spring. (It is not yet clear whether the eggs overwinter or whether the young hatch in the burrow and remain there through the winter. Overwintering as an egg would be a unique strategy for egg-laying lizards.) Gila monsters are incredibly well adapted to their arid environment and can get virtually all the water they need from their prey. Not only that, but a few meals in spring can provide enough fat for an entire year, much of it stored in the reptile's chubby tail.

In Sonora, Mexico, Gila monsters live primarily in thornscrub. Further north, through southern and western Arizona and into the fringes of neighboring states, they prefer rocky desert scrub in foothills in winter and valley washes during the warmer months, moving between them according to season and often returning to the same burrows. *Heloderma suspectum* also lives in semidesert grasslands. Pleistocene fossils suggest that Gila monsters were probably much more widely distributed thousands of years ago, but the hotter and dryer climate that followed the retreat of the glaciers restricted the range of this species. Its distribution is now closely tied to landscapes with two distinct rainy seasons, with the preponderance of rain falling in summer—a pattern typical of the Sonoran Desert Region. Though fairly common in some parts of its range, populations of *H. suspectum* are declining due to habitat conversion for development and agriculture, road construction, and illegal collection. They are protected in the states where they occur. In fact, the Gila monster was the first venomous reptile to be protected in the United States.

John N. Agnew
Gila Monster
acrylic, 24" x 18"

CAREL P. BREST VAN KEMPEN
MEXICAN BEADED LIZARD
acrylic, 20" x 30"

MEXICAN BEADED LIZARD
Heloderma horridum

At more than 2 feet in length, this is, indeed, a lizard of studded skin that can make you bristle with fear! The Mexican beaded lizard is one of only two significantly venomous lizards in the world, along with the Gila monster. Both evolved in the tropical regions of Mexico. While the Gila monster extended its territory north into the Arizona Upland subdivision of the Sonoran Desert, the beaded lizard remains closer to its roots in southern Sonora, Mexico, and in tropical deciduous and thorn-scrub habitats of Mexico and Guatemala (although it is sometimes found in pine-oak forest). Mexican beaded lizards are active during the day, primarily spring through fall, even climbing trees for food or safety, but with porous skin better adapted to their ancestral home, they avoid high temperatures that would lead to dehydration. Like Gila monsters, they pass almost all of their time in burrows.

Bony nodules or scales covered with skin create the patterned "beadwork" that decorates its upper body. *El escorpion,* as it is also called, is less brilliantly colored than its northern cousin, but its pattern of yellows and black serves well as camouflage in dappled shade, while announcing due warning to predators when it is in open areas. Although it is believed that every bite by a beaded lizard delivers toxins, unlike rattlesnakes, these venomous lizards bite only for self-defensive, causing immediate excruciating pain that imprints repulsion of beaded lizards in aspiring predators. But venom is not part of *Heloderma horridum's* own predatory strategy. Instead, it hunts eggs and slow-moving newborns, using a highly developed sense of smell. Newborn rabbits and rodents are occasional fare, but beaded lizards almost never eat quail hatchlings, because quail can run as soon as they hatch, and while the stout legs of the beaded lizards will power deep digging, they are not built for speed. Whatever these beaded lizards do catch, they swallow whole.

Medical scientists are interested in the Mexican beaded lizard because enzymes in its venom (and that of the Gila monster) are being researched for combating diabetes and other diseases. Though protected under Mexican and American law, Mexican beaded lizards are prize jewels for collectors, and poachers have had a serious impact in the decline of their populations. One employee of the Arizona Game and Fish Department tells of a man found asleep in his truck just south of the Arizona-Sonora border with seven Mexican beaded lizards in the back.

Medical scientists are researching enzymes in the venom of Mexican beaded lizards for their benefits in combating diabetes and other diseases.

Ramsey Canyon Leopard Frog
Lithobates chiricahuensis

In 1988, a herpetologist working in the Huachuca Mountains in southeastern Arizona observed that leopard frogs in a pool on The Nature Conservancy's Ramsey Canyon Preserve were breeding, but apparently *not* calling mates. A year later, he returned with a hydrophone that detects sound underwater and confirmed that this population of frogs vocalized while submerged. This behavior is relatively rare for leopard frogs, although one might expect it to be more common. Because the underwater call is inaudible or faint in the air, it is a convenient adaptation to escape detection by predators—of which these leopard frogs have many (everything from garter snakes, rats, and ringtails to mountain lions, black bears, and coatis; even giant water bugs and dragonfly larvae eat the tadpoles). At first, the Ramsey Canyon frogs were described as a new species, dubbed *Rana subaquavocalis,* (loosely, "frog that calls under water"); however, genetic studies later found that these *subaquavocalis* frogs were actually genetically identical to the Chiricahua leopard frog, who also called under water on occasion, it turned out. Frogs in Ramsey Canyon and adjacent canyons in the Huachucas were later found to call from above the water's surface as well.

Frogs from Ramsey Canyon and other sites in the eastern Huachuca Mountains often grow to a very large size and can completely lose their spots. This is not unique among Chiricahua leopard frogs, but these large frogs, that may be 10 or more years of age, are much more common in the eastern Huachucas than elsewhere, and may have been a factor in biologists mistakenly thinking they were a separate species. They can travel more than a mile across land and water, but usually stick close to their wetland homes. These leopard frogs can lay egg masses of more than a 1,400 eggs anytime from February to November, and tadpoles from later hatchings will overwinter before metamorphosing into frogs.

Historically, *Lithobates chiricahuensis* ranged through the mountainous regions of central and southeastern Arizona and southwestern New Mexico, as well as eastern Sonora and western Chihuahua, Mexico. The species is now listed as threatened on the U.S. Endangered Species List. The Ramsey Canyon leopard frog population, in particular, has been and continues to be the focus of conservation organizations, the Army, and state and federal agencies. Naturally occurring populations have been bolstered by the collection of eggs and the rearing of juveniles for reintroduction. In spite of these efforts, this particular population continues to decline in all but one of four canyons where it persists on the eastern slope of the Huachucas. Populations of these frogs were recently reestablished at a canyon on the western slope of the range, as well as in the San Rafael Valley. Historically, Chiricahua leopard frogs were abundant, reported from well over 400 sites in the United States, but by 2009, they were thought to exist at about 130 locations. Their numbers are still in decline, largely due to predation by introduced aquatic animals, loss of habitat, and the fungal skin disease chytridiomycosis, a bane on frogs and toads around the globe.

RAMSEY CANYON LEOPARD FROG
acrylic, 16" x 20"

JOHN N. AGNEW

San Esteban Chuckwalla
Sauromalus varius

The San Esteban chuckwalla is an uncommonly hefty lizard. Like the spiny chuckwalla, it is a giant in its genus. It can reach 30 inches from head to tail and weigh more than 3 pounds—at least twice the length and four times the weight of the common chuckwalla. It is endemic and largely restricted to San Esteban Island off the Sonoran coast in the Gulf of California, a landmass isolated for hundreds of thousands (perhaps millions) of years. *Sauromalus varius* is a good illustration of the concept of island gigantism, which holds that on islands where large mammals are absent, reptiles and birds have less competition for resources and fewer predators, and can therefore evolve to significantly larger sizes than closely related species on the continent.

A member of the family Iguanidae, this lizard is well adapted to its rocky, lava-strewn, arid-island home. Strictly herbivorous, it consumes many shrubs—including desert silverbush, rock hibiscus, and trixis—and to a lesser degree herbaceous plants, grasses, and flowers and fruits of cacti. An interesting adaptation in *S. various* is a gland along the nasal passages that processes and expels salts derived from plants they eat (although they do not eat halophytic plants). They sneeze a fluid that often leaves a crust of salt on their snout. All chuckwallas evolved with "lateral lymph sacs"—expandable storage tanks under the folds of skin along the sides of the body—which hold liquid for extended periods. Thus, water taken in during the rainy seasons of the Sonoran Desert Region is available during dry spells. The San Esteban chuckwalla tolerates extreme heat and can be active at temperatures exceeding 100 degrees Fahrenheit.

Common monikers for *S. varius* are the "painted" or "piebald" chuckwalla, and its characteristic mottled gray and earth-tone skin serves well as camouflage. "Retreat, hide, and don't budge" is its major defensive strategy. Confronted by predators, it will bustle into a deep cranny between rocks or boulders and balloon its body with air until it is tightly wedged, effectively preventing people or animals from pulling it out. It is interesting to note that one of its major predators has been the Seri (Comca'ac) people of the Sonoran coast, who harvested them for food, and whose oral histories suggest that they may have carried this giant chuckwalla to one or more of the other islands where it is now found (including Lobos, Pelicanos, and Alcatraz).

The most endangered of the five chuckwallas, it was listed by the United States as a foreign endangered species in 1980, and is protected by CITES. Nonetheless, nonnative animals introduced on the islands—including rodents that eat lizard eggs, and feral dogs and cats—have reduced San Esteban chuckwalla populations, and poaching for consumption or pets has also been a problem. The Arizona-Sonora Desert Museum has had a captive breeding program for the San Esteban chuckwalla since the late 1970s, which serves as a "captive assurance population" and also provides chuckwallas for other zoos. In addition, in Punta Chueca (on the coast of Sonora) an interpretive exhibit promotes the appreciation and protection of this species.

CAREL P. BREST VAN KEMPEN
SAN ESTEBAN CHUCKWALLA
acrylic, 30" x 20"

Sea Turtles

For those of us who are not connected to salt water by virtue of residence, passion, or profession, the five species of sea turtles that navigate the Gulf of California may look like minor variations on a theme. On close inspection and greater familiarity, however, the distinctions become clear, not just in form, but also in niche, and in their unique ecological services. Hawksbill turtles feed on sponges, opening forage areas for fish; loggerheads prefer molluscs and crustaceans. Leatherbacks eat jellyfish, which helps maintain fish populations, since jellyfish consume fish larvae. This Goliath of sea turtles (leatherback shells can reach 6 feet in length) also holds the record for the deepest known dive by a reptile—an astonishing 1,230 meters. Dinner for the olive ridley turtle (the smallest of the Gulf's sea turtles, reaching less than 2½ feet) also consists of invertebrates, but it forages opportunistically and can inhabit open deepwater habitats or bays and estuaries. The black turtle, an eastern Pacific variant of the circumtropical green turtle, forages on algae and seagrass, effectively grooming beds of seagrass, restoring light and a healthy environment for fish and invertebrates that use seagrass as nurseries for their young. It is the only herbivorous species.

One feature they all share is the long migration between nesting and feeding grounds. All but the olive ridley navigate across the Pacific, the Atlantic, or both. Loggerheads migrate across the Pacific from Japan, where they are born, to Baja California waters. After reaching maturity they return to Japan, remaining there to live and nest every few years thereafter. The Gulf populations of the olive ridley will travel from their mass-nesting beaches to oceanic foraging grounds more than 2,000 miles away from the coast. All these sea turtle species have a relatively wide distribution across the globe; most are found from marine regions as distant as East Africa, Brazil, Western Australia, or India, and some (like the green turtle and loggerhead) in the Mediterranean, and in the Galapagos (the hawksbill and green turtle).

Another condition these turtles share is their imperiled population status, with the Pacific olive ridley and loggerhead falling in the "threatened" category of the Endangered Species List, and the hawksbill and leatherback in the "endangered" category. Green turtles are listed as "threatened" globally; however, those populations of Pacific Mexico and in waters around Florida are listed as "endangered." The Pacific population of loggerheads has dropped more the 80 percent in the last few decades, and the Pacific leatherback may be the most critically endangered population of marine turtles on Earth, with likely fewer than 1,000 adult females alive today. The hawksbill has been the only source for "tortoise shell" glasses, jewelry, and inlays on various products, and its population has been devastated by the commercial trade. Threats common to all the turtles include nets and long-lines of a commercial fisheries industry that is dragging its feet on measures to exclude them from "bycatch" kill. Pollution, beachfront lighting, and coastal development have also taken a toll on nesting and feeding habitats of all the turtles. Fortunately, in 1990 Mexico closed once-legal turtle fisheries, which spurred a recovery for devastated sea turtle populations. In 2010 the U.S. government prohibited importation of wild-caught shrimp from Mexican waters due to lax oversight of bycatch reduction measures that impact sea turtle populations. Hopefully, this ban will help bring about more effective regulation and enforcement to benefit the sea turtles of the Sea of Cortez.

From upper right, clockwise:
loggerhead *(Caretta caretta)*
olive ridley *(Lepidochelys olivacea)*
hawksbill *(Eretmochelys imbricata)*
black turtle *(Chelonia mydas)*
leatherback *(Dermochelys coriacea)*

SEA TURTLES
watercolor, 16" x 20.5"

RACHEL IVANYI

Sonoran Tiger Salamander
Ambystoma mavortium stebbinsi

At home in ciénegas, ponds, and springs of grassland/oak-juniper habitats, the Sonoran tiger salamander never strays far from water. As with frogs, the life cycle of this salamander includes a metamorphosis from waterbound larvae to terrestrial adult. But unlike frogs, they don't necessarily metamorphose into terrestrial adults (many do not), and thus some tiger salamanders reproduce while still in the aquatic stage, continuing throughout life as gilled adults where water is perennial. In their terrestrial form, these amphibians can be dark-skinned with irregularly configured light patterns and/or spots, or they can sport large distinct yellow spots. They typically measure between 3 and 6 inches in length.

Laid in large masses, their eggs hatch into legless young in just a few weeks; the hatchlings will sometimes metamorphose in just two months or so. Not surprisingly, larval salamanders eat plankton—microscopic aquatic animals and algae. As adults (aquatic or terrestrial), they will eat larger invertebrates and insects. More surprising, perhaps, is the fact that during breeding season, they will also consume other salamander eggs and larvae. Metamorphosed adults sometimes burrow into loose soils or move into any empty burrow to avoid exposure to extremes of heat and cold.

There are two subspecies of tiger salamanders (*Ambystoma mavortium*) native to the Sonoran Desert Region—the Arizona (*A. mavortium nebulosum*) and Sonoran (*A. mavortium stebbinsi*) tiger salamanders—and both are imperiled on several fronts. First, the total population for the entire species (including the barred tiger salamander, a nonnative subspecies now present here) is already quite small—estimated to be less than 100,000 individuals globally. As the groundwater and streams of Arizona have diminished over the last century, so too have the ciénegas, ponds, and springs that supported communities of this species. In the San Rafael Valley and nearby areas, where Sonoran tiger salamanders are endemic, many natural water sources have been displaced by cattle tanks, which can dry up during droughts or erode in flood conditions. Populations of the Sonoran tiger salamander have also been attacked by a lethal virus that can be carried by people or cattle. In addition, this salamander is vulnerable to predation by nonnative fish, bullfrogs, and crayfish. Finally, the nonnative species of salamander is known to hybridize with Sonoran tiger salamander populations.

Land in the San Rafael Valley is owned primarily by federal and state entities, with a small number of private landowners, some of whom hold grazing permits and oversight of cattle ponds. Conservation easements protect small sections of the valley, one of which harbors habitat suitable for *A. mavortium stebbinsi*, but this will not be enough to keep this tiger salamander from extinction. Federal regulations may be an important factor in its continued survival.

As the groundwater and streams have diminished over the last century, so too have the ciénegas, ponds, and springs that supported communities of this tiger salamander.

Michael James Riddet
Sonoran Tiger Salamander
acrylic, 16.5" x 12.5"

Tarahumara Frog
Lithobates tarahumarae

Until the early 1980s, in the Santa Rita Mountains of southern Arizona, a hiker walking along a stream or pool might have heard a series of short snores signaling the presence of a Tarahumara frog. Or the sound might have been one of the other distinctive squawks, whines, or "eeps" they can produce without the help of a vocal sac. With luck, the hiker might have caught a glimpse of this webfoot, which resembles the leopard frogs of the Sonoran Desert Region. Although more brown in tone, the Tarahumara frog can have an olive green cast and has vague dark splotches on its back. Adults can reach 4½ inches in length; in fact, the spotted tadpoles can exceed 4 inches in length. Perhaps in part because of the Tarahumara frog's larger size and in part because dark bands mark the hind legs of both species, it is sometimes mistaken for the wetland bully, the American bullfrog introduced from the central or eastern United States many years ago and since become a major pest. But the Tarahumara frog is smaller than its bullfrog cousin, which measures up to 8 inches. Primarily nocturnal, adult Tarahumara frogs eat invertebrates like waterbugs, beetles, and hornets, and occasionally small vertebrates such as turtle hatchlings and snakes.

First described in 1917, the Tarahumara frog inhabits rocky plunge pools in canyon streams within oak or pine-oak woodlands, as well as in Sinaloan thornscrub and the fringe of the tropical deciduous forest. Until the early 1980s, they ranged from the Santa Rita, Atascosa, Pajarito, and Tumacacori Mountains in southern Arizona and in a wide corridor encompassing the Sierra Madre Occidental and associated sky island ranges in eastern Sonora, western Chihuahua, and northern Sinaloa. But by 1983 this species had been extirpated from Arizona, and several populations that once lived in northern Sonora have since disappeared. They are thought to have succumbed to a combination of environmental assaults, including the fungal disease chytridiomycosis, predation by introduced animals like green sunfish and bullfrogs, and possibly air pollution with acid rain, which can leach cadmium and other heavy metals associated with mining into the pools these frogs inhabit. Today, the frog is most abundant in the mountains of eastern Sonora, including the 70 square miles protected as a private jaguar preserve south of the confluence of the Ríos Aros and Yaqui.

In the United States, federal and state agencies have worked with the Arizona-Sonora Desert Museum and other private institutions to collect *Lithobates tarahumarae* eggs from healthy populations in Mexico for rearing, captive reproduction, and reintroduction. Frogs from this program were released into Big Casa Blanca Canyon in the Santa Ritas in 2004, 2005, and 2006, and the population reproduced well in spite of floods and fire until 2007. Then they were struck by chytridiomycosis, possibly weakened by concurrent environmental assaults and cold temperatures. As of this writing, the species had not been seen in the Big Casa Blanca area since late 2009. However, frogs introduced from the same genetic stock are surviving well in the Castle Dome Mountains near Yuma. Perhaps more exciting, tadpoles from near Yecora, Mexico, are being grown out in facilities at the Arizona-Sonora Desert Museum. This Mexican population has persisted in spite of the presence of chytridiomycosis in the area for nearly two decades. If this group of frogs is naturally resistant to the disease, their progeny will have a better chance of surviving when they are released into natural areas in Arizona.

MICHAEL JAMES RIDDET
TARAHUMARA FROG
acrylic, 16" x 12"

TRUE FROGS
Lithobates spp.

Frogs, as we know them, have been on Earth more than a hundred million years. For countless millennia, they have been ubiquitous across most of the globe, and storytellers of many cultures have honored them, as well they should. The almost magical metamorphosis from gelatinous egg mass to waterbound tadpoles to landed, air-breathing adults is enough to awe those who know their story, but they have also been a favorite food source for man and animal alike for eons. Like most amphibians, frogs expend less energy than most other terrestrial vertebrates to produce their body mass, and are therefore especially adept at transferring the energy of small invertebrates, especially insects, into energy for larger animals.

Each frog rendered on the opposite page illustrates one of more than 700 species in the genus *Lithobates* (previously *Rana*), in the order Anura. From top to bottom they are: *Lithobates blairi*, the plains leopard frog; *L. pipiens*, the northern leopard frog; *L. tarahumarae*, the Tarahumara frog; *L. chiricahuensis*, the Chiricahua leopard frog; *L. yavapaiensis*, the lowland leopard frog; *L. onca*, the relict leopard frog; and the Ramsey Canyon leopard frog, a population of *L. chiricahuensis* that was until recently thought to be a distinct species. Native to North America, leopard frogs (the "*Lithobates pipiens* complex") have slim waists and smooth olive or brown skin with dark spots. The brown singleton in the illustration, *L. tarahumarae*, is not a leopard frog. All the *Lithobates*, however, have long, strong hind legs that can propel them away from danger in a few rapid jumps, or across land during migrations from one home site to another. In these portraits, the poses speak to their nocturnal routines—some sit in wait for mate or meal, while others glide or float in the water, and another seems to climb onto a rock or bank. In breeding season they will grunt, croak, snore, or cluck to attract a mate.

Five of the six species represented here are native to the Sonoran Desert Region. Natural populations of the relict leopard frog, which was found historically in drainages of the Colorado River in northern Arizona, are now largely limited to the Lake Mead National Recreation Area. The population of *L. onca* is now so low that the survival of the species is in jeopardy. The Tarahumara frog has also disappeared from Arizona, and both of these species are now only present in the state at reintroduction sites. Furthermore, populations of the other four species are so low that their survival into the next century in Arizona is in question.

Like many other frog species from the tropics to temperate lands, these true frogs are losing their natural habitat. Loss of ponds, ciénegas, and springs, as well as extended drought, the use of cattle tanks, and the introduction of American bullfrogs and other nonnative predators have dealt a hard blow to these species. Introduced bullfrogs, which have few natural controls outside their native range, have ravaged native frogs and other aquatic animals in the Southwest, and only with intensive effort—including sharpshooters with guns—have wildlife experts made meaningful strides in eradicating these invaders. In addition, because all *Lithobates* have permeable skin, these frogs are also more susceptible to pollution and acid rain than other animals. An apparently introduced fungal disease, chytridiomycosis, has also plagued many populations of true frogs in this region.

RACHEL IVANYI
TRUE FROGS
watercolor, 20" x 9"

Top to bottom:
plains leopard frog *(Lithobates blairi)*
northern leopard frog *(L. pipiens)*
Tarahumara frog *(L. tarahumarae)*
Chiricahua leopard frog *(L. chiricahuensis)*
lowland leopard frog *(L. yavapaiensis)*
relict leopard frog *(L. onca)*
Ramsey Canyon leopard frog *(L. chiricahuensis)*

> THE STATE OF ARIZONA CAME CLOSE TO LOSING ITS STATE FISH—THE APACHE TROUT.

APACHE TROUT AND GILA TROUT
Oncorhynchus apache and *O. gilae*

Members of the salmon family (Salmonidae), Gila and Apache trout swim small, gravel-bottomed streams in the White Mountains of Arizona. The Gila trout, the one with smaller spots in this watercolor, is also found in mountain streams of southwestern New Mexico. In the wild, *Oncorhynchus apache* and *O. gilae* grow to between 9 and 11 inches—large enough to be coveted for human consumption.

Once a reliable source of protein for Native Americans, Apache and Gila trout populations fell dramatically after settlers from the East overwhelmed their capacity to reproduce in sustainable numbers. Spurred by the decline of native trout, resource management agencies began to stock nonnative species—including brown, brook, rainbow, and cutthroat trout—in those same streams, which exacerbated the decline. The nonnatives preyed on the natives and competed for their natural prey, while the rainbow and cutthroat also interbred with the Gila and Apache trout. Livestock grazing and forestry practices of the early 1900s also contributed to the degradation of their stream habitats, stripping creekside vegetation, which eliminated shade, lowered mayfly and caddisfly forage, and contributed to erosion of stream banks.

The state of Arizona came close to losing its state fish—the Apache trout. By the mid 1950s, only 30 of 820 miles of stream in Arizona were still occupied by Apache trout. In 1955, when it became evident to the White Mountain Apache Tribe that their namesake fish was on the brink of extinction, they denied fishing access on all reservation streams that supported the species. More than a decade later the Gila trout was added to the first Endangered Species List—a member of the "class of 67." Since then, federal and state agencies have had some success in recovery efforts. Today, 28 populations of Apache trout exist on the Fort Apache Indian Reservation and in Apache-Sitgreaves National Forest. With breeding, stocking, habitat improvement, and other measures, its population has increased slightly. Gila trout populations have also stabilized, but neither is out of danger, and climate change hovers ominously.

"Arizona Trout"
watercolor, 20" x 22"

Rachel Ivanyi

Desert Pupfish and Quitobaquito Pupfish
Cyprinodon macularius and *C. eremus*

The Mighty Mouses of fresh-water fish, desert pupfish and Quitobaquito pupfish only grow to 2 inches or so at maturity, but they are peerless in many respects. Robustly shaped with lips that protrude for foraging, these pupfish are exceedingly adaptable in their natural environment; they can withstand water of 110 degrees Fahrenheit or more, as well as rapid temperature swings of up to 30 degrees. They also tolerate low oxygen levels in the water, and a range of salinity from fresh water to water twice as salty as the ocean—a feat few other fish can claim. But if they are eminently adaptable, they are also adorable. Silvery with dark bands, mature males take on a light blue to turquoise iridescence in breeding season, while the tail turns yellow to rich red-orange—an attractive garb to the female's eye. The male and female perform a little courtship ritual, after which she releases eggs one at a time, each being directly inseminated by the male.

Males will stake out and defend one to two meters of river or pool bottom during the breeding season and will valiantly watch over the eggs. Omnivores, these pupfish forage for insect larvae, small crustaceans, aquatic plants, and algae. They actively dig pits into mud to find food, and there is some evidence that desert pupfish can burrow into mud and go dormant in winter. Though birds, mammals, and even aquatic insects prey upon them, desert pupfish can live up to two years, while Quitobaquito pupfish can live up to three years.

Schools of desert pupfish once wiggled abundantly through ciénegas, springs, streams, and the shallower waters of rivers in southern Arizona and southeastern California, as well as in Baja California and Sonora, Mexico (including the Santa Cruz, San Pedro, and Salt Rivers, and the lower Colorado south to Sonora and Baja California, and areas in the Salton Sea). But *Cyprinodon macularius* can no longer be found naturally in the wild in Arizona, and its populations have dwindled to a few locations in the other regions. Though desert pupfish once lived in balance with native populations of Gila chub, speckled dace, and the desert sucker, it has few defenses against nonnative mosquitofish, largemouth bass, and tilapia species that have been introduced in much of their former range. In addition, depletion of springs and pools from surface diversion and groundwater pumping has dried up countless riparian areas in the last century. Conversion of lands to agricultural use and the spraying of pesticides have also contributed to their decline. Researchers estimate that only 5 percent of former pupfish habitat remains. Quitobaquito pupfish, *C. ermeus,* have always been limited to the springs in Organ Pipe Cactus National Monument and the nearby Río Sonoyta (a Sonoran river now on verge of "extinction"), but its populations have also fallen significantly. Both species are critically endangered. In addition to its Endangered Species Act protection in the United States, the Mexican government has provided legal protection for pupfish since 1991.

Desert Pupfish can no longer be found naturally in the wild in Arizona, and its populations have dwindled to a few locations in other regions.

Rachel Ivanyi
Desert Pupfish and Quitobaquito Pupfish
watercolor, 17" x 28"

Fishes of the Colorado River

Hundreds of years ago the Colorado River and its tributaries harbored a menagerie of fish uniquely adapted to its turbulent, flood-prone waters. Each species evolved characteristics attuned to its own niche. Some, including the bonytail chub, humpback chub, and razorback sucker—two minnows and a sucker respectively—developed a hump above the snout. It is especially prominent in the humpback chub and razorback sucker. This rise functions like a keel on a boat, slicing the water and providing direction in rapid water flows. The Colorado pikeminnow and the woundfin, also minnows, lack the hump. The woundfin evolved a different adaptation—barbels, those whiskerlike projections near the mouth that hold taste buds, which help it find food in cloudy waters. The pikeminnow did not need the function of the hump since it patrols the backwaters of its riverine habitat, rather than strong currents. At no more than three inches, the woundfin fits our stereotype of the little minnow, but an adult pikeminnow will measure 3 feet or more in length (and historically reached 6 feet). It is the largest minnow in North America. The razorback sucker also grows to 3 feet, while the bonytail and humpback grow to less than 2 feet. The larger fish are relatively long-lived (between 30 and 50 years) while the little woundfin lives about four years.

Endemic to the Colorado River basin, the razorback sucker evolved here over the last million years or so, according to fossil records, and it was historically abundant. Settlers in the region pulverized this sucker to use as fertilizer for their crops or feed to their livestock. The settlers, themselves, enjoyed the taste of the Colorado pikeminnow, which they called "white salmon." All five of the species in this painting were once plentiful, but populations of each have toppled far enough to be listed in the United States as endangered or threatened. At the turn of the twenty-first century, the total adult razorback sucker population was thought to be less than a few thousand. Lower water flows and water temperature changes brought about by damming and diversion of water on the Colorado River and its tributaries have altered much of the historical habitat for all the native fish. Pollution has also increased in these waterways. One of the most significant assaults on these fish, however, has been the introduction of nonnative species to these rivers. Over the years, wildlife agency programs and private citizens introduced some 40 nonnative fish species into the Colorado River and its tributaries, creating untenable competition. These introduced fish, such as sunfishes, catfishes, mosquitofish, and nonnative trouts and minnows (e.g. red shiner), have had a significant impact, preying on the larvae and young of the natives and vying for their food. Exotic crayfish have also contributed to the decimation of native fish populations. In the last few decades, a number of government agencies and private organizations have been working to stabilize populations of native fish, but significant recovery has been elusive.

RACHEL IVANYI
"FISH OF THE COLORADO RIVER"
watercolor, 37.5" x 17.5"

Top row, left to right: humpback chub *(Gila cypha)*, bonytail chub *(Gila elegans)*, razorback sucker *(Xyrauchen texanus)*
center: woundfin *(Plagopterus argentissimus)*
bottom: Colorado pikeminnow *(Ptychocheilus lucius)*

Fishes of the Gila River

Although its common name suggests otherwise, the Gila topminnow does not belong to the Cyprinidae, or minnow family, like the other three in this painting. This topminnow belongs to the Poeciliidae, the family commonly known as "live-bearers." Smaller than the loach minnow (up to 2 1/3 inches) and the spikedace (up to 3 inches), its diminutive 2-inch length may account for the "minnow" in its name. Of the four species depicted on the opposite page (top to bottom, the Gila topminnow, spikedace, loach minnow, and Gila chub), only the Gila chub regularly grows to more than a few inches, reaching 6 or 8 inches, males and females respectively. The smaller fish occupy streams with riffles and runs, feeding along the bottom. The larger chub likes deeper, calmer pools, like those created by beavers in centuries past. Each works a slightly different aquatic niche, but all these fish share significant loss of habitat in the Gila River watershed.

At one time the Gila River watershed supported abundant populations of these and other native fishes in its various wetland habitats. They ranged from perennial marshes, springs, and seeps, to cold, quick streams at low to mid elevations (1,000 to 5,000 feet) amid pines in the mountains, and warm, sand- or gravel-bottomed streams running through cottonwood-willow galleries in grassland or desert.

In Arizona, New Mexico, and northwestern Mexico, the four native fish species rendered here once ruled the streams, springs, ponds, and ciénegas. But dams have altered the flood regimes that scoured the stream bottoms and created the perfect habitat for these species to spawn and feed. Overdraft of water directly from the Gila River or from groundwater that feeds it, the downcutting of stream channels caused by overgrazing, degradation of bank vegetation and the grasslands that retain and recharge water in the soil, and the stocking of predatory and competing nonnatives have together conspired to nearly decimate the populations of these native fishes. Nonnative fish like red shiner, western mosquitofish, sunfishes, bass, and nonnative catfishes have created havoc with native fishes in lower-elevation streams. At higher elevations, nonnative rainbow and brown trout impinge on native fish populations. For the natives, habitat has been reduced to 20 percent or less of their historical range. Although public and private efforts have been made to reintroduce native species (the topminnow has been reintroduced in nearly 200 locations), altered and reduced habitats continue to hamper recovery.

Fish of the Gila River

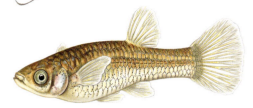

GILA TOPMINNOW
Poeciliopsis occidentalis occidentalis

RACHEL IVANYI
"FISH OF THE GILA RIVER"
watercolor, 15" x 30"

SPIKEDACE
Meda fulgida

LOACH MINNOW
Tiaroga cobitis

Gila topminnow (*Poeciliopsis occidentalis*)
spikedace (*Meda fulgida*)
loach minnow (*Tiaroga cobitis*)
Gila chub (*Gila intermedia*)

GILA CHUB
Gila intermedia

Rachel Ivanyi 2009

Yaqui chub *(Gila purpurea)*
Yaqui sucker *(Catostomus bernardini)*
Mexican stoneroller *(Campostoma ornatum)*
Yaqui catfish *(Ictalurus pricei)*
beautiful shiner *(Cyprinella formosa)*
Yaqui topminnow *(Poeciliopsis occidentalis sonoriensis)*

FISHES OF THE RÍO YAQUI

From increasingly intermittent headwaters in the San Bernardino Valley of southeastern Arizona to the sands of the Sea of Cortez, the Río Yaqui winds nearly 300 miles through arid lands. Yaqui chub, Yaqui sucker, Yaqui catfish, Yaqui topminnow, Mexican stoneroller, and beautiful shiner once navigated those vital blue ribbons in abundance. The shiner and Yaqui catfish also thrived in the Mimbres River in New Mexico, while the stoneroller navigated streams in southern Texas.

These six species range widely in size—from 2½ to 19 inches (Yaqui topminnow 2½, beautiful shiner 3, Mexican stoneroller 4½, Yaqui chub under 6, Yaqui sucker 15, and Yaqui catfish 19 inches); but all gravitate to the shade and protection of aquatic or streamside vegetation during the day, and feed on algae and detritus. Some of them also prey on aquatic insects, crustaceans, and various larvae. One—the Yaqui topminnow—boasts an unusual piscean reproductive strategy in that the male fertilizes the female ova internally instead of fertilizing an egg mass deposited by the female in the water. The female carries the developing embryos internally, and the young are born live. Only about 3 percent of fish species give live birth.

Not so many years ago, the San Bernardino Valley consisted of well-watered meadows, lush with sacaton, flowing creeks, ponds, ciénegas, and springs, but as people settled in the area in the late 1800s, they pumped groundwater and redirected pond and stream waters to their farms and livestock, eventually decreasing both surface flows and the groundwater table. In many places, cattle hooves stripped shade-producing grasses, forbs, and shrubs from stream banks and other land-water margins, leaving the native fish bereft of needed shade. Overgrazing of rain-absorbing grasslands exacerbated floods and increased erosion and downcutting of riverbanks. Drought, too, has factored into to a lowered water table, while the stocking of nonnative fish—including red shiner, green sunfish, largemouth bass, and nonnative catfish—compounded the assaults. Western mosquitofish introduced in the 1920s preyed not only on mosquitoes, as managers intended, but also on the young Yaqui topminnow, leading to a sharp drop in that species, while nonnative bullfrogs aggressively devoured and devastated myriad native fishes in the San Bernardino Valley. In the Río Yaqui watershed in Mexico, where water pollution has been an added pressure, each of the species portrayed in this painting has also declined significantly.

Native populations of beautiful shiner, Yaqui sucker, and Yaqui catfish in Arizona have already been extirpated, although efforts have been made to reintroduce some of them in the San Bernardino Wildlife Refuge, which was established in part to provide safe harbor for these fish. In both the United States and Mexico, they are all listed as rare, threatened, or endangered.

Rachel Ivanyi
"Fish of the Río Yaqui"
watercolor, 22" x 18"

MICHAEL JAMES RIDDET
HUACHUCA GIANT SKIPPER
acrylic, 9" x 12"

THE HUACHUCA GIANT SKIPPER IS THOUGHT TO HAVE AS FEW
AS 20 REMAINING POPULATIONS IN SOUTHERN ARIZONA.

HUACHUCA GIANT SKIPPER
Agathymus evansi

With a wingspan between 1¾ and 2⅜ inches, this full-bodied butterfly is the largest and rarest of the Megathyminae, or giant skippers, in the large superfamily Hesperioidea. Skippers (Hesperioidea) are distinct in the shape of their antennae, which have the clubbed tip bent slightly backwards. Because skippers share the robust thorax and have proportionately smaller wings than other butterflies, they can easily be mistaken for moths. The "skip" in the common name refers to the brisk pattern of their flight. The adult butterfly does not eat or visit flowers, but the males seek water in mud or moist sand and are reported to sometimes drink liquids they have eliminated from their own bodies. Males are not quite as large as females and have smaller and more yellow than yellow-orange spots.

Agathymus evansi is known only from mixed pine-oak-juniper woodland habitats between 5,600 and 5,800 feet in the Huachuca Mountains of southern Arizona. Although some sources suggest they may occupy similar sky island habitats in Sonora and Chihuahua, Mexico, records are unavailable to confirm these reports. Adults fly mainly in September and October, but unlike the famous monarch, they do not migrate, maintaining close proximity to Huachuca agave, their larval host plant. Females drop their eggs on this agave's succulent leaves. After hatching, the caterpillars bore in about halfway up the leaf, where they feed on the pulp until they are ready to hibernate in the fall. In spring they inch down to the base of the leaves and feed on sap until summer, when they aestivate. Before it pupates, the caterpillar covers the opening of its tunnel with silk.

The Huachuca giant skipper is thought to have as few as 20 remaining populations in southern Arizona. Both catastrophic wildfire and overgrazing are threats to this skipper. Although it has not been listed as endangered by federal or state agencies in the United States, the Forest Service considers this butterfly a sensitive species and NatureServe Explorer lists it as imperiled.

Aquatic Invertebrates

The gleaming shells and curious dry structures spiraling through this painting were once living animals—mobile, moist, and vital on a wet canvas of tidepool or river bottom: sea urchins, murexes and other snails, sand dollars, chitons, pitars, mussels, clams, oysters, and other bivalves. Each of these species is an invertebrate (animals lacking backbones), and they all make their living in complex aquatic ecosystems. All but the California floater, a freshwater mussel, are important primary consumers of algae or other small invertebrates in or near tidepools of the Sea of Cortez (Gulf of California), where they are inextricably linked to, and necessary for, a healthy functioning marine ecosystem.

While the empty shells gain aesthetic accolades, these creatures have myriad, largely unknown, underappreciated virtues that captivate the imagination. For example, chitons (fourth from the center), are ancient molluscs dating to at least 500 million years ago that have multiple rows of teeth, many of which are coated with magnetite, a surface purportedly harder than stainless steel. They are unique in their ability to produce significant quantities of this mineral. Sand dollars are a kind of "flattened sea urchin" that make their living capturing plankton on their mucus-coated shell; there are three beach-drift, pale, dry "tests," or skeletons, of sand dollars in this painting. But in life, they are dark purple and densely covered with tiny spines and short tubelike feet with which they ambulate on the soft sea bottom. Microscopic grooves move plankton—like algae, various larvae, and detritus—along a ciliary-mucus conveyor belt to a central mouth. Cowries are herbivorous sea snails that work near the low-tide line, using their toothed tongues to scrape algae off rocks and ledges. They continually polish their own shell by the use of highly extensible lobes, called the mantle.

Each of the salt-water species illustrated here has been extirpated from broad areas of their former range by the degradation of coastal habitats along the Sea of Cortez (e.g., beachfront housing, resort and marina construction, shrimp farm construction, etc.), by exploitive or careless fishing practices (e.g., shrimp trawlers that destroy the seabed), and by over-collecting by tourists and shell-trade professionals. The freshwater outlier in this painting—the California floater (twelfth from the center)—once lived in nearly every river in Arizona; indeed, Native Americans and pioneers throughout the West harvested them for food. Today, the Arizona population is restricted to a short stretch of the Black River, in the east midsection of the state. Freshwater mussels (*Anodonta* and similar species) were abundant all over North America a century ago, but like the California floater they are now absent from most freshwaters in the United States. In fact, freshwater bivalves (clams) are among the most threatened animals in the world. The same massive extirpation has occurred with freshwater bivalves in Europe.

Shells, from center out:
(1) Test (skeleton) of slate pencil urchin (*Eucidaris thouarsii*), (2) Moon snail (*Polinices recluzianus*), (3) Test (skeleton) of juvenile sand dollar, (4) Gulf chiton (*Chiton virgulatus*), (5) Slate pencil urchin (*Eucidaris thouarsii*), (6) Tower shell (*Turritella gonostoma*), (7) Annette's cowrie (*Cypraea annettae*), (8) Gulf pitar (*Pitar vulneratus*), (9) Purple dye snail (*Plicopurpura patula*), (10) Spiny pitar (*Pitar lupanaria*), (11) Chestnut cowrie (*Cypraea spadicea*), (12) California floater (*Anodonta californiensis*), (13) Amathusia venerid (*Chionopsis amathusia*), (14) Santinada clam (*Flabellipecten sericeus*), (15) Test (shell) of giant sand dollar (*Encope micropora*), (16) Pink murex (*Chicoreus regius*), (17) Tent olive (*Oliva porphyria*), (18) Black-skinned Panamic whelk (*Pleuroploca granosa*), (19) Test of Gulf giant keyhole sand dollar (*Encope grandis*), (20) Black murex (*Chicoreus nigritus*), (21) Panamic pearl oyster (*Pteria sterna*), (22) Pacific lion's paw (*Nodipecten subnodosus*).

SCOTT FRASER
SHELL SPIRAL
oil, 24" x 36"

ABERT'S TOWHEE
Pupil aberti

A plain brown songbird, Abert's towhee stays out of the spotlight as much as possible, spending much of its time tracking down seeds, grubs, and adult insects under dense shrubby growth. Like other towhees, it uses its thick legs and claws to scuff through leaf litter, kicking up these edible delectables. *Pupil aberti* is large for a member of the sparrow family, at 8 or 9 inches in length and approaching 2 ounces. It is distinguished by a distinct black face and black feathers about its beak, as well as the sound of its call—a series of peeps punctuated by quick chirps. Abert's towhee does not migrate or otherwise fly long distances, but sticks close to its breeding territory. Although the term for a group of towhees is "a tangle of towhees," this particular species is not normally seen in groups; it is a solitary bird.

Abert's towhees keep the same mate for several years, and perhaps for life, maintaining year-round territories. The parents weave open-cup nests out of grass blades, bits of forbs or vines, and other plant materials, and produce 2 to 4 eggs per clutch. However, their nests are choice targets for nonnative cowbirds, which often toss one of the towhee eggs out of its nest to lay their own egg in it, and the towhee parents unwittingly raise the cowbird chick. This brood parasitism may have contributed to a decline in Abert's towhee populations in the last century. However, nesting two or three times over a long breeding season appears to be one of this towhee's strategies to keep its genes moving along in the avian world. They nest with the rains, sometimes as early as March, and then again, once or twice, until the rains are over in August or September.

Habitat loss has contributed to declines in *P. aberti* populations. It is endemic to the watersheds of the Gila and Colorado Rivers, mainly in southern and western Arizona, as well as a bit of western New Mexico and small patches of Utah, Nevada, and California where those states border on Arizona. It is one of the most limited distributions of any bird species in the United States. As a riparian obligate fond of dense thickets along perennial streams and urban habitats in the lowland deserts, its populations have suffered with the drying of rivers due to drought, groundwater pumping, and water diversion, as well as degradation or loss of streamside vegetation from uncontrolled grazing. The Audubon Society reports that when cattle were removed along the 40 miles of Arizona's San Pedro Riparian National Conservation Area in the late 1980s, the Abert's towhee population rebounded within five years. Ornithologists believe that *P. aberti* may be at close to 50 percent of its historical population.

ABERT'S TOWHEES ARE CHOICE TARGETS FOR BROOD
PARASITISM BY NONNATIVE COWBIRDS.

ABERT'S TOWHEE
oil, 12" x 16"

JOE GARCIA

Bald Eagle
Haliaeetus leucocephalus

In the United States, images of the bald eagle are ubiquitous. Ben Franklin's preference for turkeys notwithstanding, the choice of *Haliaeetus leucocephalus* as this country's national bird was not entirely ill-conceived. With its superior size and strength, this accipiter has been simultaneously respected and dreaded. Even its appearance inspires awe. Its large head, deep feathered brow, and sharply hooked beak suggest fearlessness, if not ferocity. Its snowy white head and dark brown body suggest it does not rely on camouflage, reinforcing the perception of boldness and underscoring the eagle's position as an apex predator.

Bald eagles, like osprey, live around significant bodies of water, and are thus rare in arid lands. Bigger than osprey, adult bald eagles can measure 3 feet or more in length and weigh up to 10 or 14 pounds, males and females respectively, with wingspans of 6 or 8 feet. Not only do they use the same water-dominated habitat as osprey, they compete for the same prey and often snitch food outright from their smaller cousins. Primarily piscivores, they also eat whatever the occasion presents—including small mammals, reptiles, and birds—hunting in full sunlight or in the penumbra of dawn and dusk. They are also willing to eat carrion. Bald eagles typically build nests on cliff ledges or in tall conifers or deciduous trees—nests that measure several feet wide and deep, as you might expect of one of the largest and heaviest birds in North America. While courting, the male and female perform an acrobatic free fall from a high altitude, somersaulting talon to talon. As a rule, bald eagles mate for life, and under good conditions they can live 30 years.

Historically, bald eagles ranged across North America, from Canada to Mexico, but in the twentieth century, thousands of these raptors (and others) across the continent died from hunting, DDT poisoning, habitat conversion, and other anthropogenic causes. By 1963 they had been extirpated from the majority of the United States. Once the U.S. government listed *H. leucocephalus* as endangered in 1967 and the use of DDT had been banned, most of the bald eagle populations recovered remarkably. However, the Sonoran Desert population is still highly vulnerable to disturbance and habitat loss, and while bald eagles were removed from the U.S. Endangered Species List in 2007, the Sonoran Desert population was reinstated as threatened in 2008. This population is limited to central Arizona, and Mexico's northwestern coast. The Verde River has been a primary nesting area for the Arizona population, which is estimated at fewer than four dozen breeding pairs.

EDWARD ALDRICH
BALD EAGLE
oil, 16" x 20"

Cactus Ferruginous Pygmy Owl
Glaucidium brasilianum cactorum

Its long common name reflects its most salient characteristics. "Cactus" speaks to its preference for nesting in cavities excavated by flickers or woodpeckers in saguaros or other columnar cactus; the Latinate "ferruginous" describes the iron-rust color of its body and tail bars (although this subspecies can vary to paler and more gray); "pygmy," of course, refers to its diminutive size (an average 6½ inches in length and 2½ ounces). Finally, it is a "true owl" (as opposed to a barn owl)—a subspecies of one of more than a dozen *Glaucidium* species in the family Strigidae.

It may be small, but this little raptor can be ferocious—at least one researcher dubbed it "the terror of small birdlife." It will hunt mourning doves and other birds more than twice its size, swooping low to the ground to seize the prey with its inordinately large talons. It can hunt any time of day or night, but is mainly crepuscular, most active at dawn and dusk when more insects, lizards, birds, rodents, and other prey species are active. Although most owls fly silently, the wingbeats of a cactus ferruginous pygmy owl are audible, which may account for their preference for a perch-and-wait or short-flight hunting strategy. The characteristic disc shape of the plummage around the owl's eyes helps in the hunt by directing faint noises to its ears, while binocular vision helps it pinpoint prey. It is itself prey to hawks and other raptors. In the Sonoran Desert Region, this owl usually lives in areas with mesquite, ironwood, or cottonwood trees—often riparian woodlands or washes in desert scrub and semi-desert grasslands, places where cacti or trees provide nesting cavities. In their far southern range they occupy thornscrub or deciduous forest.

Glaucidium brasilianum cactorum was once common from south-central Arizona to Sonora and Sinaloa, Mexico, but populations have declined on both sides of the border—more drastically in Arizona. Here, cactus ferruginous pygmy owls are now largely limited to the Altar Valley and an area northwest of Tucson, and fewer than 40 individuals per year were recorded in Arizona between 1996 and 2009, a number so low that many biologists doubt it will survive in this area. Unfortunately, its habitat often coincides with choice land for residential development. In Mexico, too, it is losing ground. There, much of its habitat has been aggressively converted to agricultural and livestock use, including intentional seeding of the invasive, nonnative buffelgrass, which engenders more frequent and high-intensity wildfires that kill the columnar cacti and trees the owls live in. A quarter of the population of cactus ferruginous pygmy owls in Mexico had already been lost by the first decade of the twenty-first century. Since the species has no protection in Mexico, further losses are expected. In the United States this pygmy owl was listed in 1997 as a federally endangered species. Despite a recommendation from the Fish and Wildlife Service to retain its protection, it was delisted in 2006 following protests from industries invested in land development.

Rachel Ivanyi
Cactus Ferruginous Pygmy Owl
watercolor, 16" x 20"

California Brown Pelican
Pelicanus occidentalis californicus

The California brown pelican is a very big bird, the largest subspecies of the wider-ranging brown pelican. Mature birds measure about 4 feet in length and weigh in around 8 pounds. Their wingspan can reach 7 feet; the bill alone, about a foot. The fossil record tells us that its form has changed very little over tens of millions of years. The large size of this bird's bill and throat pouch was heralded long ago in a popular limerick by Dixon Merrith, and it is true that its "beak" will hold more than its belly can. Indeed, its pliant pouch can hold well over twice the volume of its one-gallon stomach. Unlike the white pelican, the brown pelican dives steeply into the ocean to feed, scooping up small fish, or occasionally squid and other invertebrates. John Steinbeck described the manner of their "clumsy-appearing" dive as "folding their wings and falling," but noted it must be effective if the birds thrived—which they did until the second half of the twentieth century.

Flying in formation, flocks of brown pelicans have long skimmed the sea along the Pacific Coast of California from the Channel Islands to Baja California, and down the shores of western Mexico to the Tres Marías Islands north of Puerto Vallarta. Breeding in colonies, they tend to build flat clumsy nests, often on the ground, out of sticks, preferably on islands. Outside of breeding season, many will migrate further north along the California coast or to the inland Salton Sea. Rarely, they drift into the arid lands of Arizona, along the lower Colorado River. Both males and females will incubate their eggs, not by sitting on them but by standing on them with their great webbed feet. This curious behavior contributed to the bird's steep decline in the 1960s, when heavy use of the pesticide DDT caused their egg shells to thin, making them easily crushed by parental attentions. A healthy California brown pelican can live about 25 years.

In 1970, on the brink of extinction, brown pelicans were listed as endangered under the U.S. Endangered Species Act. Although the species has made a remarkable comeback with the banning of DDT, and was taken off the Endangered Species List in 2009, these sea birds are still susceptible to environmental assaults. They are sensitive to pesticide residues in fish they eat, and they are susceptible to loss or degradation of roosting and breeding habitat, like mangroves, and to boating and poaching in their nesting areas. Overfishing of sardines or anchovies—their preferred food—may impact populations of the California brown pelican, and infectious diseases brought about by the crowding of these birds in commercial fish dumps and in boat marinas is also a concern.

"High Flying Brown Pelicans: Where the Desert Meets the Sea"
oil, 16.5" x 20.5"

Janet Heaton

Edward Aldrich
California Brown Pelican
oil, 26" x 19"

California Condor
Gymnogyps californianus

The humongous size and pink skinhead of the California condor evoke images of prehistoric creatures. In fact, *Gymnogyps californianus* is a direct descendant of Pleistocene ancestors. Up to 500 years ago, California condors were plentiful in North America. Averaging about 20 pounds, with a wingspan approaching 10 feet, this is the continent's largest flying terrestrial bird, and it can fly at speeds up to 50 miles per hour. It may look like a fearsome beast, but it is not the dirty killer nineteenth-century settlers mistook it for. Even into the late twentieth century, many ranchers assumed condors had slaughtered the rotting carcasses they ate, causing aggressive retaliation for its presumed "take." In fact, condors do not kill. They are exclusively carrion-eaters. Neither are they "unclean"—they wipe their faces on grass or other rough surfaces after eating, bath often, and preen their feathers regularly. When not under assault by human activities, they can live 45 to 50 years. Unfortunately, California condors have been actively hunted, shot, or poisoned since settlers first arrived, and by the mid-1900s this giant pacifist was speeding toward extinction. Condors appeared on the first U.S. Endangered Species List in 1967.

By 1987, only 22 California condors still lived. These last condors were captured for a captive rearing program, from which juveniles would be released back into the wild. But because they naturally hatch only one egg every two years, and because they are not sexually mature until they are five to seven years old, re-establishing a viable population has been exceedingly slow. The first group of condors was reintroduced in 1992, and by early 2010, 187 condors had been released into the wild, with the total captive and released population at about 350 birds—still perilously close to the brink. Condors favor cliffs and shallow caves for nest sites, and the Grand Canyon (where their ancient bones have been found in caves) now harbors almost a third of the reintroduced condors. The coastal mountains of California support most of the rest, with other refugees making a living in the Sierra San Pedro Martir of northern Baja California. A partnership of private and public entities in the United States and Mexico are working to rear, introduce, and manage the wild and captive populations.

Unfortunately, recovery has been crippled by ongoing anthropogenic activities. Nearly 40 percent of the reintroduced condors have either died (from poaching, poisoning, or electrocution on power lines) or were returned to captivity to treat inflictions. Wild hatchlings are not common, and several wild hatchlings have perished from consuming human trash. In addition, California condors are especially sensitive to lead due to their stomach acids, and lead shot in the carcasses they scavenge continues to be a major cause of condor death. Continued loss of habitat is also a concern. Although the number of condors has increased since the captive breeding program began, NatureServe Explorer notes "the increase occurred as a result of intensive management rather than from natural population growth." The California condor is still one of the most critically endangered animals in the world.

California Condor
acrylic, 27" x 22"

Carel P. Brest van Kempen

> The overwhelming threat to least Bell's vireo is the disappearance of low, dense riparian vegetation, much of which has been lost to stream overdraft, development, grazing, and other anthropogenic causes.

Least Bell's Vireo
Vireo bellii pusillus

Small and drab, in tones of gray, the least Bell's vireo isn't usually thought of as an avian celebrity. It is often described as "nondescript," and though technically a songbird, it sings a phrase some call "unmusical." Its size, at just 4 to 5 inches, also doesn't pull much weight (in fact, it is only 9 grams). Like all birds, however, it evolved within a given habitat with characteristics and behaviors that enabled it to survive. So far, at least.

Vireo bellii pusillus is a subspecies of the more widely distributed Bell's vireo, largely limited to southern California and the Baja California peninsula where they breed in the north and winter in the south. It is a bird of arid lands, adapted to low, dense brush and streamside thickets. While it will snatch some prey in the air, this vireo usually picks its food from leaves and bark, either holding onto or hovering in front of trees and shrubs; insects (lots of beetles, moths, and caterpillars) and spiders make up almost the entire diet of least Bell's vireo, though fruit and snails are also on its menu. It builds a pendulous nest in the crook of a branch, usually less than three feet off the ground in a bush or small tree—often a type of willow. The nest is camouflaged with bark, grass, and foliage. Despite its size, the least Bell's vireo will defend its nest vigorously against intruders, although predators—everything from western scrub-jays, Cooper's hawks, raccoons, coyotes, and gopher snakes, to various rodents—often have their way.

The influx of cowbirds into the Southwest, however, presents a bigger threat than predators. This nonnative species lays one or more eggs in the vireo's nest, and the unsuspecting parents will raise the firstborn cowbird at the expense of their own offspring. But the overwhelming threat to least Bell's vireo is the disappearance of low, dense riparian vegetation, much of which has been lost to stream overdraft, development, grazing, and other anthropogenic causes. Cowbird parasitism only exacerbates recovery by hampering the vireo's reproductive success, and the little vireo has been extirpated from 95 percent of its historic range. Its population in the United States had dropped to a precarious 600 individuals in 1986, when *V. bellii pusillus* was first listed as an endangered species, but by 2009 that population had increased to more than 6,000, mainly due to efforts in California to control cowbirds and protect or restore habitat. A few hundred birds still reside in Baja California, Mexico. There is hope for a stable population; but habitat protection and restoration will be critical.

MICHAEL JAMES RIDDET
LEAST BELL'S VIREO
acrylic, 16" x 20"

Masked Bobwhite
Colinus virginianus ridgwayi

A subspecies of the northern bobwhite, the masked bobwhite is one of the least quail-like members of the New World quail family Odontophoridae, measuring between 8 and 10½ inches in length. Its elegant plumage is a variegated combination of rust, chestnut, buff, black, gray, and white—bars, bands, patches, and zigzags. The males, whose black hood is unique to this genus, can be heard whistling something that sounds like "bob-white," prompting its common name. These handsome birds inhabit open desert grasslands, semi-arid desert scrub, and valleys or bottomlands. Here, they find a good mix of grasses, herbs, and forbs that provide seeds to eat from fall through early spring (when they particularly favor seed from the whiteball acacia tree). In summer and early fall, they feed on insects and green plant materials. Except during spring breeding season, masked bobwhites consort in coveys of up to 20 birds. In previous centuries, indigenous people and settlers may well have hunted this tasty quail, but today they are only hunted by wild predators like raptors, owls, coyotes, and other carnivores.

The ornithologists who wrote *The Birds of Arizona* described the masked bobwhite as "the first bird wiped from the face of Arizona."

> "…it had thrived in the prosperous grasslands of the border; but it died off almost instantly at the demise of its home with the coming of the great herds…. Let those who really wish to conserve our wild heritage ponder well the lesson!" (*The Birds of Arizona*, 1964)

Until the late nineteenth century *Colinus virginianus ridgwayi* ranged from south-central Arizona (mainly the bottomlands of the Altar and Santa Cruz Valleys) to central Sonora, Mexico, but by the first decade of the twentieth century they were entirely gone north of the border. This collapse is attributed mainly to the pervasive overgrazing of cattle in the late 1800s and subsequent habitat damage. Heavy grazing denudes the ground of grasses and forbs that provide cover and nesting sites, as well as food, for this species. Without the grass cover, which overgrazing removes, the land also loses the necessary fuel for natural, recurring grassland fires that stay the encroachment of scrub mesquite and other woody vegetation (which in turn displaces grasses and forbs that are resources for the quail and other grassland species). Drought and toxins may have exacerbated those problems. In 1969 the United States listed *C. virginianus ridgwayi* on its Endangered Species List, and in 1985 the Buenos Aires National Wildlife Refuge was established as a safe haven for the species. Here, a rearing and release program maintains a population of masked bobwhite, and habitat is being managed to the quail's benefit. In Sonora, Mexico, three wild populations survive, but these populations are declining. The total number of surviving masked bobwhites is estimated at fewer than 1,500 individuals, including the 300 or so at the Buenos Aires Ranch. This is one of the most threatened birds of the Sonoran Desert Region.

The total number of surviving masked bobwhites is estimated at fewer than 1,500 individuals.

Masked Bobwhite
oil, 14.5 x 18

Joe Garcia

Northern Aplomado Falcon
Falco femoralis

"Clever" would probably not be an inappropriate descriptor for the northern aplomado falcon. They often hunt cooperatively in pairs, dashing into brush and grasses to flush out prey. They also are known to follow four-footed predators as they move through grassland inadvertently raising birds and other small prey from their cover. This raptor will perch for hours in trees that punctuate open grasslands and marshes; silently they lay in wait, surveying, ready to swoop out in pursuit of a bird or rodent off its guard. It typically catches birds and insects in flight, but will also take reptiles and other small animals on the ground.

The northern aplomado falcon is easily recognized by conspicuous markings on its white face and throat, a slender body and wings, a black sash across its breast, a long black-and-white banded tail, and long legs. An adult bird may measure up to 16 inches in length, and about 3 feet from one rounded wingtip to the other. Although a broad-brush map of its current geographic distribution still paints most of its historic range—from the extreme southwestern United States to southern South America—its presence within that vast range is now spotty. A small area in north-central Chihuahua, Mexico, still harbors *Falco femoralis*, but this bird has disappeared from most of northern and central Mexico. In recent decades, it was seen rarely in the San Rafael Valley of Arizona, in isolated parts of southwestern New Mexico, and in parts of Texas.

Northern aplomado falcons were fairly common until the late 1880s, but by the 1930s, the species had been virtually extirpated from its northern range. At one time, it shared habitat with black-tailed prairie dogs; but when prairie dogs in the region became a perceived nuisance to the ranching industry in the early twentieth century, the U.S. government worked to eliminate them, using various poisons, including strychnine. When the prairie dog population had been purged, the northern aplomado falcon was also gone. Toxins that worked their way through the food chain are thought to have killed falcons, but other factors are also implicated in their disappearance. Because aplomado falcons do not build their own nests, using abandoned nests of other species, the death of other raptors would also reduce available nest sites. In addition, the invasion of brush and scrub mesquite due to overgrazing and drought has changed the character of its open habitat in the borderlands region. While DDT probably did not play a large role in the decline of this accipiter in the United States, it has caused eggshell thinning in aplomado falcons in eastern Mexico. And at the turn of the twenty-first century, birds in the lower Rio Grande and other parts of south Texas were found to contain PBCs, heavy metal, and organochlorine pesticides. Texas Parks and Wildlife reports, "This group of pesticides has been linked directly to the deaths of thousands of songbirds, waterfowl, and raptors in Argentina and parts of the United States."

Before and after its listing as endangered in 1986, reintroduction programs by private conservation organizations and public agencies released several dozen aplomado falcons in Texas. They are reproducing and will hopefully establish a viable population if habitat is protected and environmental contaminations are controlled.

NORTHERN APLOMADO FALCON
oil on linen, 28.5" x 22.5"

LARRY FANNING

Osprey
Pandion haliaetus

Osprey soar while they hunt for the slippery denizens of lakes, rivers, and coastal marshes. Unlike other raptors, they catch fish by diving from high above the water, almost straight down, at the last moment throwing their feet forward to capture a fish in their sharp talons. Well adapted for this job, osprey have little spines called spiricules on the soles of their toes, and one of the three front toes can reverse direction to create two sets of opposing toes. Combined with the strength of their claws, these features give them the needed edge over hard-to-grip fish. Also known as fish hawks, osprey are, indeed, mainly piscivores, but they will also eat crabs, birds, and other small vertebrates. As adults, they weigh about 4 pounds and measure close to 2 feet in length. They can be distinguished from other raptors in flight by their white underside, narrow wings (nearly 6 feet from tip to tip), and black patches at the wrist joint, where the wings bend.

Osprey are a cosmopolitan species, breeding from eastern and western Canada to Florida, Baja California, and Guatemala, and while those in the northern United States typically winter in northern South America, some in the Sonoran Desert Region will stay throughout the year. They weave rough nests on tall trees or other projections near water, (including snags, rocks, telephone poles, and other manmade structures), returning to the same nest for several years. During mating season, males declare their nesting territory and solicit females with a ritual "dance," beating their wings rapidly and rising steeply to hover with tails splayed broadly. They will cry out, diving and hovering repeatedly, sometimes holding fish or sticks. Osprey courtship also includes feeding the mate.

In the mid to late twentieth century, widespread populations of osprey were threatened by the build-up of DDT pesticide in the food chain. Populations of osprey are now fairly secure, but in much of the Sonoran Desert Region and surrounding states its breeding status is vulnerable. This may be due primarily to the association of osprey with declining water habitat, but the osprey entry in the 1964 publication, *Birds of Arizona*, is revealing. "How this magnificent hawk can survive in Arizona is a marvel, considering that even fish-and-game rangers are instructed to shoot them on sight. Man cannot tolerate an animal that is a better fisherman than he is!" Although attitudes have changed within game-and-fish departments in recent decades (with more effort expended toward conservation), in some places antagonism lingers toward wild creatures who compete with us for natural resources—an attitude that still factors into the decline of large predators, whether bird or mammal.

In some places antagonism lingers toward wild creatures who compete with us for natural resources.

EDWARD ALDRICH
OSPREY
oil, 12" x 24"

Michael James Riddet
Rufous-winged Sparrow
acrylic, 16" x 14"

Rufous-winged Sparrow
Aimophila carpalis

The rufous-winged sparrow was first recorded near Tucson, Arizona, in 1872—one of the last birds to be described in the United States. Though considered shy, this small passerine bird perches and builds nests toward the outer edges of trees or shrubs, where it can be easily observed. About 5 inches long and a full half ounce, it can be distinguished from other members of the sparrow family (Emberizidae) by its rust crown and eye-line, and the conical yellow beak flanked by two black "whiskers" on each side. One striking, and obvious, feature of this songbird is the common closing to its various songs, in which a single high-pitched *"seep"* is followed by an increasingly quick succession of abbreviated chirps. Its most familiar melody is said to have a mournful tone.

The limited geographic range of *Aimophila carpalis* is represented on maps as a long wedge with its head in south-central Arizona, tapering down along the mainland Mexican coast through southeastern Sonora to a point in central Sinaloa, across from the tip of Baja California. Traveling through this territory in fall or winter, you might see a flutter of rufous-winged sparrows as they gather in family flocks. In the Sonoran Desert, they are found in relatively flat lowlands with bunch grasses (like sacatons), small thorny trees and shrubs (like mesquites and hackberries), as well as chollas and other cacti. Resident year-round, they do not need to drink free water, obtaining what moisture they require from the food they eat. Just the same, this sparrow depends heavily on summer rains for successful nesting. The parents can raise broods two or three times in a year, but without good rains they may not breed at all. On the ground or in shrubs, *A. carpalis* forages for grasshoppers, caterpillars, and other insects during the warm months and relies on seeds throughout much of the year.

Shortly after the species was first recorded, it was described as common in south-central Arizona. But this bird makes use of a habitat that in recent decades has been heavily converted to residential, commercial, and agricultural use. So, although they are not locally uncommon today, their limited range and the significant reduction of appropriate bunch-grass and thornscrub habitat makes them a species of concern. Overgrazing and urban development has resulted in the degradation of much of their habitat—as well as that of Brewer's, chipping, and black-throated sparrows. Although most rufous-winged sparrows live in the wilds of Sonora, Mexico, little is known about their situation there; we do know that loss of this habitat type has also been significant south of the U.S.-Mexican border.

Thick-billed Parrot
Rhynchopsitta pachyrhyncha

Striking to the eye and caustic to the ear, thick-billed parrots are conspicuous in brilliant green plumage with vermillion accents on the forehead, eyes, shoulders, and thighs. A vociferous bird about 16 inches in length, its loud, harsh shriek can sometimes be heard more than a mile away. Natives of ancient cultures and European settlers of the nineteenth century who lived near the sky islands of the Sonoran Desert would have been hard-pressed to misidentify this species. In past centuries, these parrots flew as far north as the Verde River; at least as late as 1935, and possibly 1945, they were seen in the highlands of southeastern Arizona. Thick-billed parrots are social nomads known to flock in companies of up to 1,000 individuals, traveling wherever conifer tree cones are edible and plentiful, flying long distances in a wedge. (The V-formation reduces air drag for those birds in the wing wake of the bird ahead, conserving energy and thus extending the flight.)

Of all the New World parrots, only *Rhynchopsitta pachyrhyncha* occupies mature or old-growth temperate forests. They favor conifer forests, pine and fir as well as mixed pine-oak woodland, from 3,900 to a cold 11,500 feet. (They have been seen eating snow, presumably to get water). They eat pine nuts, primarily, harvesting them from the cone systematically in a spiral progression—a behavior that must be taught to young parrots. They will also eat acorns and Douglas fir seeds, as well as berries.

While parrots no longer reside in or visit the mountains of Arizona, they still survive in parts of the Sierra Madre Occidental in Mexico, although most of the old growth forest there has been cut down for timber or pasture. Habitat loss across its former range has been devastating—fewer than 4,000 individuals are thought to survive anywhere. In 1964 the authors of *Birds of Arizona* opined, "Because of the rapid destruction of the pine forests of Sonora and Chihuahua, this parrot will probably never be seen again in Arizona." In the 1980s a small population of captive-reared and wild-caught thick-billed parrots were released in the Chiricahua Mountains, where they had once been abundant; but many of those birds lacked defensive skills and were taken by predators (hawks, falcons, and ringtails); others were inefficient foragers, and the reintroduction effort failed. Fortunately, two National Forest Reserves have recently been established in prime thick-billed parrot habitat in the Chihuahuan highlands of Mexico.

Edward Aldrich
Thick-billed Parrots
oil, 24" x 12"

While parrots no longer reside in or visit the mountains of Arizona, they still survive in parts of the Sierra Madre Occidental in Mexico.

ADELE EARNSHAW
VIOLET-CROWNED HUMMINGBIRD
oil on birch, 20" x 24"

VIOLET-CROWNED HUMMINGBIRD
Amazilia violiceps

A rare sight in the United States, the violet-crowned hummingbird is the only hummer in North America with a clear white chin, breast, and belly. This fact, coupled with its blue-purple crown and long, nearly straight red beak with a dark tip, make it easy to identify. (Males and females are almost identical, although the female's crown is duller.) Relative to others in the family Trochilidae, the adult is large—about 5 grams (a little more than a sixth of an ounce) and all of 4 inches. Like other hummers, violet-crowned hummingbirds have great stamina and aerial talent; their broad, flat, pointed wings—which are connected just at the shoulder—allow them to rotate their wings and create "lift" in any direction. They can fly at high speeds, hover, and move up, down, or backwards, which allows them to be virtually still in midair to drink nectar from flowers (and makes it easier for them to escape from predators). In order to fuel their aerobatic maneuvers, they drink from flowers with a high percentage of nectar sugar, which provides calories. For protein and other nutrients, these hummingbirds snatch small insects in the air. In addition, they conserve energy by resting on a branch most of the day, making only quick jaunts to forage. At night, or under duress, they can go into a state of torpor, lowering their heart rate and energy needs.

During the summer mating season, the chatter of violet-crowned hummingbirds might be heard in open woodlands along the eastern border of Sonora and in the Madrean Highlands of Chihuahua, Mexico, as well as in the sky islands of southeastern Arizona (primarily the Chiricahua and Huachuca Mountains, rarely along Sonoita Creek), as well as around Guadalupe Canyon in southwestern New Mexico. Some birds winter over in the breeding range, and violet-crowned hummers have been found as far north as Tucson in winter, but most winter in Mexico, ranging through a broad band down the Pacific slope in southern Sonora that broadens and veers away from the coast toward the interior as it extends to northwestern Oaxaca.

Because *Amazilia violiceps* prefers to nest in the branches of large riparian trees, especially Arizona sycamore, drought and continued loss of riparian habitat factor into the viability of this species in its remaining territory in the United States, as well as in the desert scrub and thornscrub of Mexico. In its southernmost range, it commonly nests in smaller oaks. Because of its high need for energy, necessitating access to hundreds of flowers each day, drought and degradation of riparian corridors clearly impacts populations of violet-crowned and other hummingbirds.

Western Burrowing Owl
Athene cunicularia hypugaea

THOUGH ITS DISTRIBUTION IS WIDE, THE OCCURRENCE OF THIS WESTERN BURROWING OWL IS INCREASINGLY SPOTTY, AND SCIENTISTS ESTIMATE IT HAS LOST MORE THAN 60 PERCENT OF ITS HISTORIC BREEDING POPULATION.

With its blunt head, big round eyes, and full body, the western burrowing owl looks a lot like other birds in the family Strigidae, a family known as "typical owls." But this one is not your typical hooter. With atypically long, nearly featherless legs, it regularly runs across open areas chasing large insects (like scorpions, crickets, and wolf spiders), small mammals, reptiles, or amphibians. It can also fly to chase insects, bats, and birds. These terrestrial and airborne animals are standard dietary fare for many other owls, but the cholla and prickly pear fruit that the omnivorous burrowing owls also savor are not. Unlike most owls, this species hunts both day and night, depending on the nature of the prey, and it evolved a clever food-gathering strategy—luring dung beetles to the dinner plate by distributing mammal droppings around the burrow. One of the smallest in North America (with a mature adult of 10 inches in length weighing about 6 ounces), western burrowing owls are themselves prey for foxes, coyotes, hawks, and great horned owls, among others. Barring natural, vehicular, or environmental assault, they can live about ten years in the wild.

Athene cunicularia hypugaea nests not in trees or cactus, but underground in dens. Although they are capable of digging their own lair in certain soils, they usually use those dug by prairie dogs, banner-tailed kangaroo rats, foxes, tortoises, ground squirrels, or other burrowing animals. When excited or agitated, they will bob their heads or whole bodies up and down, often calling out

"EYE TO THE SKY" ANNE PEYTON
acrylic, 28" x 24"

WESTERN BURROWING OWLS
acrylic, 15" x 25"

RICHARD SLOAN

with a short "chuck"—a call specific to predator warnings. Its territorial call sounds like a high-pitched "hoo hoo." Burrowing owls will perch in the open on dirt mounds, rocks, or trees, and seem to be less skittish of people than most owl species. They will sometimes settle near golf courses, farms, or similar urban or exurban developments.

Western burrowing owls prefer dry, open land, whether prairie, grassland, or desert. They are found from the grassland regions of Canada through the United States west of the Mississippi, and south through Mexico and western Panama. Those in the northern range are breeding migrants, but many are permanent residents in the Sonoran Desert Region and further south. Though its distribution is wide, the occurrence of this subspecies is increasingly spotty, and scientists estimate it has lost more than 60 percent of its historic breeding population. The United States government has recognized *Athene cunicularia hypugaea* as a "candidate species" for the Endangered Species List, while the Canadian government considers them endangered. Habitat loss or degradation constitute the greatest threats to this species. The campaign against prairie dogs, coupled with residential and agricultural development, and the use of pesticides, particularly threaten the survival of the western burrowing owl.

Western Yellow-billed Cuckoo
Coccyzus americanus occidentalis

The western yellow-billed cuckoo is a Neotropical migrant songbird, a term applied to birds with a melodious call that migrate back and forth annually from more topical climes in South or Central America to breed and nest in North America during the warmer seasons. This particular songbird belongs to the family Cuculidae; it is a subspecies that likely differentiated from the eastern yellow-billed cuckoo more than 200,000 years ago. Averaging 12 inches in length, adults have a yellow ring around each eye and a de-curved, dark-blue-upper and yellow-lower bill (a bill longer and heftier than in the eastern yellow-billed cuckoo). Seldom on the ground, this short-legged bird nests and forages in dense foliage, staying largely out of sight.

In the Sonoran Desert Region, western yellow-billed cuckoos are one of the last migrants to arrive, typically not until June or early July, after which they mate, incubate, and nurture their young to fledging before heading south again between late August and mid September. True to their name, they evolved some distinctive behaviors. In courtship, the male offers a tail-flicking female a twig, which she takes in her beak, and which they both hold as they mate. In addition to laying in their own well-hidden (but poorly built) nests, western yellow-bill cuckoos will sometimes lay eggs in a neighbor's nest—nests of either their own species or others. Although hatchlings emerge from the pale, green-blue shells shut-eyed and featherless, their feathers virtually pop until, within two hours they are entirely feathered. The next day, the newborns can eat whole insects. (Caterpillars, especially sphinx moth larvae, and grasshoppers make up the bulk of the western yellow-billed cuckoo diet, but they sometimes gobble flies, beetles, and other insects, and rarely a frog or small lizard). A week or so after hatching, the chicks start scrambling up the branches and, amazingly, a few weeks later are ready for the long southward migration.

In the Sonoran Desert Region, where heat and aridity factor into survival, *Coccyzus americanus occidentalis* nests in riparian corridors, preferably in cottonwoods or willows over open water, and preferably in closed-canopy gallery forests (which provide greater humidity in and below the canopy). Coincidentally, these birds reportedly raise their long, cadenced call more frequently on overcast or cloudy days (another condition corresponding to higher humidity), so much so that another common moniker for this species is "raincrow."

Historically widespread from the Rockies to the West Coast, from Canada to Sonora, this subspecies of cuckoo has undergone a drastic range reduction, and is now breeding primarily in Arizona, and while still present in some California drainages, its numbers have been drastically reduced. The conversion of riparian forest to agricultural land, stream channeling, and the invasion of the tamarisk tree and other exotic plants have taken a toll. Populations of a few dozen to a couple hundred breeding pairs are still found in California, in western New Mexico on the Rio Grande, and in northern Mexico. They have been completely extirpated from Alaska, British Columbia, Washington, and Oregon. Ornithologists estimate that their populations have declined by 90 percent since the late nineteenth century, which matches the approximate loss of natural riparian habitat in Arizona over the last century or so. Fewer than several thousand adult birds are thought extant. Unfortunately, breeding populations of western yellow-billed cuckoos require not just a few trees, but between 25 and 100 acres of mature riparian forest. It has been a qualified candidate for the Endangered Species Act since 2006, but has not been listed due to priority status of so many other endangered species. So many species to save; so little time.

Michael James Riddet
Western Yellow-billed Cuckoo
acrylic, 17" x 23"

BLACK-FOOTED FERRET
Mustela nigripes

This black-masked rascal is a member of the weasel family (Mustelidae), along with mink, fisher, skunk, and other species with glands that produce a musky odor. Of three ferrets worldwide, the black-footed ferret is the only North American species. It is thought to have evolved from Old World ferrets that arrived on this continent in the late Pleistocene by way of the Bering Land Bridge. Eventually, black-footed ferrets found an abundant source of food among millions of prairie dogs whose abandoned burrows also provided ready-made homes, and in time prairie dogs became the ferret's near-exclusive prey.

With short strong legs, sharp claws, and a keen sense of smell, ferrets have no trouble navigating dark tunnels to ambush sleeping prairie dogs, and their nocturnal forays skirt the problem of prairie dog sentinels. Ferrets, themselves, are prey for coyotes, foxes, raptors, and badgers. Adults are small and slender, weighing between 1½ and 2½ pounds, and measure up to 18 inches in length, not including a 5- or 6-inch tail. They run up to 7 miles an hour, not by strides, but by repeated jumps. Young ferrets, like many young mammals, are particularly energetic and playful, wrestling and rolling around with each other, and ferrets of all ages "dance" by hopping and bucking wildly about!

Black-footed ferrets once thrived from southern Canada to northern Mexico, encompassing a swath of the continent between Montana and North Dakota that broadens to the south from Arizona to Texas. This species came within inches of extinction in the late twentieth century, mainly as a result of prairie-dog-control campaigns by the U.S. government and the livestock community. They also succumbed to the introduced sylvatic plague that wiped out many prairie dog communities, a disease that transfers readily to ferrets when they feed on infected prairie dogs.

In 1985, only 18 black-footed ferrets lived anywhere on Earth; they were survivors of the last known community of *Mustela nigripes*, a population in Wyoming that had collapsed after the introduction of canine distemper. These 18 ferrets were captured to begin a captive breeding program through which at least 15 sites have since been stocked with breeding pairs, including one site in Arizona and one in Chihuahua, Mexico. By 2010, more than 1,000 black-footed ferrets had been reintroduced into the wild. While the breeding program has been relatively successful, a good-sized population of ferrets needs at least 10 thousand and probably closer to 20 thousand acres of prairie dog town to sustain it, and, in this century, prairie dog habitat is highly limited and patchy, and prairie dogs continue to be subjected to eradication pressures and habitat loss. Habitat protection will be a key to the survival of both prairie dogs and black-footed ferrets.

NICHOLAS WILSON
BLACK-FOOTED FERRET
gouache, 12" x 24"

Black-tailed Prairie Dog
Cynomys ludovicianus

Of all the animals at risk in (or already extirpated from) the Sonoran Desert Region, prairie dogs may be the ones that tug most at our hearts. Not only are these short-eared, big-eyed members of the squirrel family (Sciuridae) irresistibly cute, they also have a complex social system with parallels to our own. Like other species of prairie dogs, black-tailed prairie dogs live communally and cooperate on daily tasks like digging, sentry watch, and burrow repair. A single burrow system can cover just one acre or stretch for tens of miles. Within them, family groups called "coteries" have tunnel "property" that they defend, and sections of their burrows are specifically assigned to sleeping, food storage, rearing pups, or defecating. The coterie is generally made up of a polygamous male, his mates, and their young. In a gesture that looks like a kiss, members within a coterie touch teeth as a means of identification. They also groom and play together. Groups of coteries are known as "wards," and prairie dogs keep to their own wards. Multiple wards constitute a colony or "town." Throughout the day each coterie has a sentry who communicates to the group, using at least ten different calls. In fact, researchers in northern Arizona found that the Gunnison prairie dog has one of the most sophisticated animal languages yet deciphered. They use distinct vocalizations for coyotes, domestic dogs, hawks, eagles, and humans, and also have a grammar to describe the size, shape, and color, as well as the speed of travel for these other creatures! Adult black-tailed prairie dogs are between 14 and 17 inches long and typically weigh 2 to 3 pounds. They have white bellies, black-tipped tails, short ears, and dun-colored backs that blend well with the ground.

Prairie dog communities support dozens of other animal species that depend on them for prey or for the use of their abandoned burrows. Black-tailed prairie dogs, in particular, have been integral in sustaining the swift fox, mountain plover, ferruginous hawk, burrowing owl, various snakes, and the black-footed ferret, the last being a federally listed endangered species, largely due to the loss of *Cynomys ludovicianus*.

Prairie dogs were once ubiquitous across the West in high deserts, short-grass prairies, and open semi-desert grasslands. *Cynomys ludovicianus* is one of five species of prairie dogs that historically ranged across some 80 to 100 million acres east of the Rocky Mountains and west of the Missouri River, from southern Canada to northern Sonora and Chihuahua, Mexico, including the Great Plains. They currently occupy less than two million acres in that range, and have been virtually extirpated from southeastern Arizona and northern Mexico. They eat primarily short grasses and weeds, and some flowering plants, and are not known to need free-standing water. Though superbly adapted to their grassland habitats and ecologically successful by any measure, these intelligent, social critters have been wrongly viewed as competitors for rangeland, and were the subject of persistent eradication campaigns by ranchers with poisons and guns. Recent studies indicate they have little impact on available fodder and do not seriously compete with cattle and other range stock. In fact, their lifestyle might even increase the amount of available forage. Habitat loss has also been a factor in their decline, while an introduced flea-born plague continues to cause the collapse of large communities.

PRISCILLA BALDWIN
BLACK-TAILED PRAIRIE DOG
graphite, 14" x 17"

John Seerey-Lester
"Sonora Majesty"
oil on canvas, 24" x 36"

Jaguar
Panthera onca

Jaguars are justly extolled as feline royalty; they are the biggest, most powerful, and, arguably, the most handsome cat in the Western Hemisphere. They are the third-largest cat in the world, up to 300 pounds, and endowed with a deep, big-cat roar. *El tigre,* as it is known in Mexico, has also been justifiably feared, even the smaller jaguar of the Sonoran Desert Region. They can easily take down cattle, sheep, or other livestock, a fact that has motivated warfare by ranchers against *Panthera onca* in spite of a very low incidence of depredation. They generally consume deer, javelina, frogs, rabbits, skunks, coatis, and even some fruits. Unlike most cats, jaguars will also eat carrion.

In historic times jaguars ranged well into the Southwest and south to Paraguay and northern Argentina, including dense tropical jungles where some populations still thrive. In the last century, however—motivated by profits, fear, and competition for habitat and nature resources—people have shot, killed, poisoned, or displaced jaguars until they vanished from nearly a third of their original panAmerican habitat. In Mexico, they now occupy less than 40 percent of their historical range. *El tigre* has taken a big hit from the ranching industry, but its handsome spotted coat has also caused its slaughter. Even the black, melanistic jaguars have subtle rosettes. (Although not documented north of Chiapas, occasional anecdotal reports of black jaguar from southern Sonora persist). Like ocelots, jaguars were over-exploited for their coats. In 1968, 13,516 jaguar pelts came into the United States. Since then, most countries have banned the hunting of jaguar, but these laws are almost impossible to enforce, and while the fur trade has abated, these great cats are still being killed. At the same time, forests are being slashed and roads cut into their habitat. By 2008, only about 150 jaguars were thought to survive in the Sonoran Desert Region, virtually all of them south of the U.S. border. In recent years, however, education has been changing attitudes toward jaguars and conservation in communities in both Mexico and the United States.

Mexican governmental and nongovernmental agencies began emphasizing jaguar conservation in the late 1900s. They have been changing perceptions of the jaguar from that of "nuisance" to "partner in the ecosystem"—establishing programs in rural schools and paying ranchers for taking photos instead of killing the big cats. In the Río Aros/Río Yaqui area, binational organizations established 70 square miles of reserve lands for the jaguar and all those species protected under its umbrella—including Neotropical migratory birds, bats, butterflies, and river otters, as well as ocelots, military macaws, and bald eagles. The U.S. government listed the jaguar as endangered in 1997, and in 2010 planning began for critical habitat protection.

Today, in northern Mexico *Panthera onca* scent-marks its territory in remote pine-oak and pinyon-juniper habitat, and also in thornscrub and occasionally in coastal mangrove habitats. One considerable population stalks its prey in a remote, dry, and rugged landscape in Sonora, where thornscrub and tropical deciduous forest meet. At the beginning of the twenty-first century, at least two jaguars were marking their territory in southeastern Arizona and southwestern New Mexico; however, for jaguars, the construction of the border fence will undoubtedly cut travel corridors between the United States and Sonora.

MARTIENA RICHTER
"FOREST DWELLER"
scratchboard and watercolor, 12" x 16"

MARGAY
Leopardus wiedii

Margays are acrobatic cats. They leap easily through forest canopies, where they spend most of their time. *Tigrillos,* as they are also known, can virtually run upside down along a branch, climb down a tree face-first, hang by their strong hind claws with front paws free like a squirrel, or simply hang from a branch with one foot. Among cats, these talents are highly unusual; only the clouded leopard of Southeast Asia can compete with the margay, which evolved special adaptations in its paws to accommodate travel high in Neotropical forest habitats. Its paws are broad and large, with long claws, flexible toes, and strongly articulating foot bones (metatarsals). Amazingly, their hind paws can rotate 180 degrees.

Descended from the same ancestors, margays look like ocelots, but smaller, more slender, with a slightly different pattern of spots, a longer tail, and larger, more prominent eyes. Its ringed tail is 20 inches long—about two-thirds as long as its body—and they weigh in at around 7 pounds. Unlike ocelots, they generally take their meals in the trees, eating small animals that make a living among the foliage—squirrels, small birds, reptiles, and arthropods—as well as some fruit. Primarily nocturnal, they may den in hollow logs or burrows during the day. Although solitary, except when mating, they have a fair array of vocal communications, including purring, meowing, barking, hissing, growling, and snarling.

Most margays are found in humid tropical and subtropical forestlands, but they can also inhabit dense semiarid thornscrub and more temperate forests with extremely dense canopies. *Leopardus wiedii* ranges from southern Sonora on the west coast of Mexico (and Tamaulipas, Mexico, on the east) through Central America, and across a great swath of northern South America, including the Amazon Basin, through northern Argentina and northwesern Uraguay. One margay was collected in the lower Rio Grande Valley in Texas in the mid-nineteenth century, and they are thought to have ranged into Texas, Arizona, Arkansas, and Louisiana in the nineteenth century. Populations of margays dropped dramatically in the twentieth century, and across their broad range they are now rare. Like the other spotted cats, they have been exploited for their pelts. Consider that between 1976 and 1985, at least 125,547 margay skins were recorded in the trade (and no doubt many more went unrecorded). And margay populations are still in decline. In spite of current legal protections, poaching for pelts and the pet trade is still a major concern, but habitat loss to deforestation and land conversion is now considered the greatest threat to these unique cats.

MICHAEL JAMES RIDDET
MERRIAM'S MOUSE
acrylic, 16" x 12"

BASED ON ITS NICHE IN THE SONORAN DESERT REGION OF ARIZONA, ITS ONLY HOME NORTH OF THE BORDER, THIS MOUSE IS ALSO CALLED THE MESQUITE MOUSE.

MERRIAM'S MOUSE
Peromyscus merriami

Though commonly called a field mouse, this rodent is not in the same family as the common house mouse or other Old World species, which belong to the family Muridae. Merriam's mouse is a member of the family Cricetidae, one of 58 species of deer mice in the genus *Peromyscus,* a genus endemic to the New World, and each species is highly adapted to the ecosystem in which it is found. Based on its niche in the Sonoran Desert Region of Arizona, its only home north of the border, *P. merriami* is also called the mesquite mouse. In Mexico, its range extends through Sonora to central Sinaloa.

You can easily distinguish between field mice and house mice by the white belly and big ears of *Peromyscus*. Like many other deer mice, Merriam's mouse has a tail slightly longer than its body—4 to 5 inches of tail to nearly 4 inches for the body—which helps provide balance as it clambers through trees and shrubs for seeds, fruits, flower, greens, and insects. Active in all seasons, these nocturnal, white-booted field mice are a staple food for carnivorous mammals and birds.

Mature mesquite bosques (forests) in lowland riparian corridors, a habitat in which this field mouse evolved, are now scarce in southern Arizona. Some have been cut down for firewood, while others have died due to lowered water tables resulting from human overdrafting of groundwater. Unfortunately, this mouse is adapted to those large bosques with dense groundcover—including cacti, grasses, and other vegetation—which they use for nesting. While Merriam's mouse does not live among small scattered mesquite trees on washes, or in mesquite invaded grasslands, it will sometimes live in Sonoran Desert scrub dominated by mesquite. Although not yet officially endangered, Merriam's mouse is considered a "priority vulnerable species" by Pima County, where it was once abundant, and a "sensitive element" by the Arizona Game and Fish Department. Fortunately, mesquite forests are returning in some protected areas, such as Cienega Creek in Pima County, Arizona.

MEXICAN GRAY WOLF
Canis lupus baileyi

The story of the Mexican gray wolf is the same sad story of human and administrative ignorance, arrogance, genocide, remorse, captive breeding, and virtually futile reintroduction attempts that have plagued apex predators throughout the world. Little more than a century ago, countless Mexican gray wolves ran free in mountains, grasslands, and shrublands from central Mexico to Texas, New Mexico, Arizona, and Colorado, but today most of the surviving 300 or so Mexican gray wolves are in zoos. Indeed, the entire species *Canis lupus* has been largely extirpated throughout its historic range in North America.

As the smallest subspecies of gray wolves *(Canis lupus)*, adult Mexican gray wolves typically carry less than 100 pounds on their 3-foot frame. In the Southwest this wolf is often referred to as *el lobo*. Like other wolves, they are intelligent and social, traveling and working together in packs of a few to a dozen, more or less. The packs are made up of a life-bonded pair and some or all of their offspring. Some of their progeny leave the pack at maturity; others remain. With howls, growls, bowing, tailwagging, scent-marking, and various other vocalizations and behaviors, they communicate with each other both to hunt and to maintain order in the pack. They have great stamina, long legs, and large paws that can carry them at 30 miles an hour for short distances or, considerably more slowly, more than 30 miles over the course of a day. They will hunt a territory of hundreds of square miles if necessary, according to the abundance of deer, elk, pronghorn, and other prey. The natural history of wolves has been well documented, and the fascinating and endearing behaviors of the Mexican gray are no different from those wolves that turned Ernest Thompson Seton from a hired wolf killer into a conservationist.

Unfortunately, the story of the Mexican gray wolf is as familiar as it is tragic. Once abundant in their range, they helped keep populations of large herbivores in check, a critical function that maintains overall ecosystem health. But when settlers arrived in force from the East, many saw the wolf as a threat to livestock and livelihood, and in 1915 the U.S. and state governments, along with ranchers and bounty hunters, went to war against the wolf, using guns, traps, and poisons until, in the early 70s, the wolf's demise was clear. By that time, ecologists had gained a better understanding of the essential roles of individual species in natural food webs. Public sympathies had also been turned by a growing conservation movement. As early as 1959, the Arizona-Sonora Desert Museum made a long-term commitment to Mexican gray wolf conservation. That year, the museum was given a wolf captured near Tumacácori, Arizona. That wolf was the first of one of three genetic lineages of captive Mexican wolves in existence today. In 1975, the Museum staff was already developing plans for reestablishing Mexican wolves in the wild in the United States and supporting their continued survival in Mexico. Near extinction, *Canis lupus baileyi* showed up on the U.S. Endangered Species List in 1976, and the last five wild wolves were eventually captured for a captive breeding program. By 2008—a decade after the first releases—more than a hundred Mexican grays had been reintroduced in the Apache and Gila National Forests of Arizona and New Mexico, but nearly half had been killed, returned to captivity, or lost for various reasons. The program persists, but the challenges are great, and few places remain where these wolves are welcome.

"Mexican Gray Wolves"
oil, 20" x 30"

Larry Fanning

Mt. Graham Red Squirrel
Tamiasciurus hudsonicus grahamensis

If you hike the Pinaleño Mountains of southern Arizona in summer, just after dawn or as dusk approaches, you might see a small red squirrel skittering through spruce and fir. When these high forests turn frigid in winter, however, you would be more apt to see one in the middle of the day bustling toward its midden on the forest floor, where it will have stashed seed cones for future consumption during more productive seasons. One of twenty-five subspecies of red squirrels in North America, *Tamiasciurus hudsonicus grahamensis* is smaller than most tree squirrels, including most red squirrels, at about 12 inches in length, including its bushy tail. Although this fierce little forest denizen will chatter loud warnings and aggressively defend its midden territory from potential intruders (including its close cousins), a mother squirrel may "gift" part or all of her territory to her offspring, and the middens may be used over several generations. Sharp-shinned, Cooper's, and red-tailed hawks consider them a tasty meal, as well as an easy mark, as do other raptors like northern goshawks, spotted owls, and great horned owls. Gray fox, bobcat, and other carnivorous mammals also have a penchant for red squirrels, and thus it is not surprising that most do not survive their first year. Those that do can live about three years. They usually nest in the hollow of a tree, but some will nest in ground burrows, and some patch together a ball nest high in the limbs of a tree, using leaves, grass, and other plant materials.

Tamiasciurus hudsonicus grahamensis lives only in Arizona's Pinaleño Mountains, where it has been isolated for perhaps eight thousand years, since Pleistocene glaciers receded and a hotter, more arid climate created vast desert barriers between this sky island and other suitable habitats in the Sonoran Desert Region. Once thought extinct, Mt. Graham red squirrels were rediscovered in the 1970s. After the United States listed it as critically endangered in 1987, nearly 2,000 acres of essential habitat were set aside in the Pinaleños, habitat that included three wetland areas profiting not only red squirrels, but countless other species. (One of the great strengths of the Endangered Species Act is that protecting habitat for one species inevitably protects many other species.) This squirrel's limited range and small population alone would make the species vulnerable to extinction, but environmental and other pressures continue to hurt its chances of survival. Much of the squirrel's natural habitat was harvested for timber more than 40 years ago, restricting suitable forest lands to less than 100 square miles. In addition, the squirrel's forage within that limited range—including cones, other seeds, mushrooms, and insects—are being usurped by an introduced competitor, the Abert's squirrel. The construction of the Mt. Graham International Observatory at the end of the twentieth century also brought ecological disruptions, including fragmentation by roads and more people. Drought, fire suppression, catastrophic fire, and insect damage to the trees—including damage by an introduced beetle, a native beetle, and a native moth—have also compromised its resources. At the turn of the twenty-first century, fewer than 400 Mt. Graham red squirrels were probably left—a dangerously low number to assure survival of the subspecies.

NICHOLAS WILSON
MT. GRAHAM RED SQUIRREL
gouache, 24" x 12"

> IN THE MODERN ERA, THE SEDUCTION OF THEIR FUR
> LED TO EXCESSIVE SLAUGHTER OF OCELOTS.

Ocelot
Leopardus pardalis sonoriensis

In the southern reach of the Sonoran Desert the ocelot, or *el tigrillo,* stalks through dense thornscrub in the dark and nether ends of night, seldom hunting by day. Further north it travels through live oak scrub or the green corridors along the Río Mayo and other rivers and streams in Sonora, Mexico. Now and then it is spotted in southeastern Arizona. During the day, it will stretch its 30-pound, 3-foot frame across a tree branch for a nap, or it may retire to a rock-walled den or to the cover of thick brush. Sometimes two will travel together, but by and large they move and hunt alone. Agile and fast, the ocelot takes a broad range of prey, including javelina, frogs, fish, fawns, doves, rabbits, rodents, snakes, birds, and insects. It is also able to leap and swim well, allowing it to stay a step ahead of coyotes and wild dogs that pursue it. To escape the maw of a mountain lion, however, its sensitive ears must be constantly tuned to any rustle or scrape that might belie the presence of the bigger cat.

The elegant coat of the ocelot has been admired since prehistoric times (ocelots are also known as the "painted cat"). On each cat, the pattern is slightly different, the way our fingerprints are different. But in the modern era, the seduction of its fur led to excessive slaughter. More people, better technology, and a human penchant for exotic fashion converged to devastate many populations of all five *Leopardus pardalis* subspecies that ranged through much of Central and South America. They were hunted for the high price of their sublime coats. In the United States the genus *Leopardus* was listed as endangered in 1982, which helped change trade regulations. Now that real fur is less openly sought in developed countries and some governments have limited fur trade, pelt-hunters are less of a threat. However, trapping for pet sales has been on the rise.

Leopardus pardalis albescens still has a small population in southern Texas and eastern Mexico, where it lives in chaparral thickets that have had some protection, but habitat in Texas is being lost to development, and vehicles kill significant numbers of ocelot on the roads there. In the Sonoran Desert, on both sides of the border, ocelot territory has been seriously fragmented or converted to agricultural land. Roads here are also a problem, as is the border fence which blocks their access to forage and mates. Around the turn of the twenty-first century, before construction on the border fence began, researchers noted evidence of a slight drift north of the Sonoran ocelot into southern Arizona, in Pima, Santa Cruz, and Cochise Counties; they speculated that habitat preservation along the San Pedro River may have contributed to this movement.

Edward Aldrich
Ocelot
oil, 20" x 30"

Pronghorn
Antilocapra americana

Pronghorn are the single extant species of the unique family Antilocapridae. Though similar in appearance to antelope (and sometimes called "pronghorn antelope"), they are only distantly related to true antelopes. The fleet-footed pronghorn are endemic to North America. Just two centuries ago, they browsed in the tens of millions across the grasslands and plains from south-central Canada to southern Mexico. By 1915, however, fewer than 15,000 remained. Conservation efforts and subsequent laws and regulations slowed the tide of decline, and the population is probably close to a million pronghorn today, but they remain a vulnerable species. In the Sonoran Desert Region, in particular, the rare Sonoran pronghorn, *Antilocarpa americana sonoriensis,* is especially threatened.

Smaller than their northern cousins, Sonoran pronghorn stand approximately 3 feet high at the shoulder and 4½ feet in length, but are otherwise similar in form and markings. The tan coat, white underbelly, and white bands on the front of its neck are distinctive; in Mexico, they are known as *berrendo*, meaning "two-toned." Males generally have two-tined horns, while horns on females are smaller and unbranched. They weigh between 75 and 130 pounds, with males heavier than females.

Over millennia, these dryland pronghorns adapted well to the landscape—areas now dominated by palo verde, other small leguminous trees and various cacti, and areas where creosote and bursage are prevalent. They eat grasses, but they will also browse herbaceous plants and shrubs, as well as cacti that most grazers will not eat. In extreme heat, they can raise the hairs on their coat, allowing air to cool their skin. Wary and watchful, pronghorn always move together. They are equipped with *very* large, keen eyes set high—eyes that can rotate almost 320 degrees, allowing them to easily survey the horizon as they browse. They evolved to evade predators by flight, and healthy pronghorns can outrun any other land mammal in North America, racing in unison at speeds up to 55 or 60 miles an hour. They also stot or pronk like a gazelle, a "bravado" behavior believed to communicate their superior strength to potential predators—among them coyote and mountain lion. Indeed, they can outrun these animals over open country for great distances. Unfortunately for pronghorn, they didn't evolve with fences or other high, continuous obstructions. Unlike deer and horses, they can't jump fences. In this modern world, they are cornered.

At one time, many herds of Sonoran pronghorn grazed from the Imperial Valley in California through southern Arizona and south through Sonora at least to Hermosillo, but only three populations of *A. americana sonoriensis* still graze anywhere on this globe. The Sonoran pronghorn has been listed as endangered in the United States since 1986. One herd of about 100 individuals is located in protected areas and military land in southwestern Arizona (this group is a successfully reintroduced population); and two herds, totaling around 650 individuals, roam in the El Pinacate region, where a Mexican reserve protects their habitat. With a border fence, there will be no chance for this population to range northward in search of sparse resources (or to find new mates in the Arizona population). The American pronghorn, *A. americana,* can be seen in the grasslands around Sonoita, Arizona.

One major threat to Sonoran pronghorn is diminished water sources, due to water diversion, drought, and climate change. During the extended drought of 2002, the herd in Arizona dropped to only 25 individuals. Eventually, a captive-breeding effort reinvigorated that population. Poaching is also a concern, as are security activities along the Arizona-Mexico border and loss of habitat to agriculture and development.

PRONGHORN
gouache, 18" x 24"

NICHOLAS WILSON

Spotted Bat
Euderma maculatum

Its name, like most common names, comes from its obvious qualities; *Euderma maculatum* has three conspicuous white spots on its black fur—on the rump and on each shoulder. The back of its ears are also marked with white. But the spotted bat might well have been called the "big-eared bat," had the name not been taken. The spotted bat has the largest ears of all bats native to the United States; they are pink and disproportionately huge, measuring 1½ to 2 inches, compared to a body length of 4 to 4½ inches. Of course, acoustic reception is critical to bats, who use echolocation to navigate penumbral and black skies, and this bat prefers to fly in the middle of the night, reportedly at high speeds. They use a low-frequency echolocation call to hunt prey, a frequency that can't be heard by moths, which make up virtually all their diet. People, however, can hear this call about 800 feet away. Spotted bats emit a variety of other sounds as well, for different purposes, including high-pitched noises and a distinct clicking sound before flying.

The natural history of *Euderma maculatum* is still a bit sketchy, largely because it is rare, or rarely encountered. While their range is broad—from British Columbia, through most of the western United States and south to Durango and Queretaro in central Mexico—they are found so infrequently and in habitats so varied that, so far, most of what we know is just informed guessing. The meager evidence does provide some insight, however. Some spotted bats reside in montane habitats with mixed conifer forests and/or ponderosa pine, at least in the early summer; others are found in deserts and semi-desert grasslands, or low-elevation canyons and cliffs. Some roost in rock crevices. Though otherwise nonmigratory, some researchers speculate that these bats move from high to low elevations, depending on the season. They are generally solitary, but may gather in small groups to hibernate. Most sightings of spotted bats have occurred in California, Arizona, New Mexico, southern Colorado, and southern Utah.

The threats to this species are not well understood, but it is thought to be one of the rarest mammals in North America, and low numbers alone would make the species vulnerable to extinction. Damming canyons in the latter part of the twentieth century may have reduced preferred roosting sites, and the use of pesticides, which accumulate in prey, probably constitutes a threat.

THE SPOTTED BAT IS THOUGHT TO BE ONE OF THE RAREST MAMMALS IN NORTH AMERICA.

CAREL P. BREST VAN KEMPEN
SPOTTED BAT
acrylic, 20" x 30"

Arizona Claret Cup
Echinocereus arizonicus

Petals of saturated red, or claret color—and the striking contrast of a green stigma and yellow anthers against them—distinguish this magnificent hedgehog cactus. The flowers are also relatively large, measuring up to 2 inches in diameter, and emerge directly from the side of the plant's upper stem during the dry foresummer months in the Sonoran Desert, usually from April to May. Bees land on the stigma and dive into the tangle of anthers to gather pollen for their larvae, inadvertently fertilizing flowers as they move from claret cup to claret cup. Hummingbirds attracted by the bright red blossoms also help pollinate this plant. In May and June, spiny red fruits the size of a cherry tomato mature and are readily consumed by rodents and other desert creatures. Natural predators of the Arizona claret cup cactus are mainly insects—especially leaf-footed bugs, which suck its sap, or boring insects.

The deeply ribbed, dark-green stems of this species usually grow in clumps of a few to twenty or more, with the stems up to 16 inches tall and 4 inches or so in diameter. To tell the Arizona claret cup from other hedgehogs when it is not in flower, look for the smooth pinkish or gray spine at the center of each spine cluster; in this species the central spine grows downward, and the radial spines are slightly shorter and thicker than in most hedgehogs.

The Arizona claret cup is known almost exclusively from mountains in Gila and Pinal Counties in south-central Arizona, with patchy occurrences in other areas of the state, and in New Mexico and northern Sonora. *Echinocereus arizonicus* grows at elevations of 3,400 to 5,300 feet in canyons and on slopes where you might also find desert spoon, beargrass, point-leaf manzanita, mountain mahogany, and squawbush. It thrives among shrubs or granite boulders in semi-desert grasslands and oak woodlands.

Mining operations and off-road vehicles both pose a threat to this rare cactus, which was registered on the Endangered Species List in the United States in 1979. At the end of the last century, its population was estimated at only about 1,000 individual plants. The taking of Arizona claret cup is prohibited in Arizona and it is protected from international trade, but illegal collection of these attractive cacti still constitutes a threat.

THE SPINY RED FRUITS OF THE ARIZONA CLARET CUP CACTUS ARE READILY CONSUMED BY RODENTS AND OTHER DESERT CREATURES IN THE EARLY DESERT SUMMER.

ARIZONA CLARET CUP CACTUS CONSTANCE SAYAS
watercolor, 12" x 24"

BOBBIE BROWN
BRISTOL'S HEDGEHOG CACTUS
watercolor, 22" x 20"

BRISTOL'S HEDGEHOG CACTUS
Echinocereus bristolii

This perennial succulent is one of dozens of species of hedgehog cactus (a name derived from its resemblance to the prickly Old World animal of the same name). A dense coat of spines helps protect it from the maws of herbivores and also provides a modicum of shade from the intense summer sun of the Sonoran Desert Region. This particular hedgehog has light green stems, which are usually solitary or branched near the base when they are young. As the plants mature they may cluster in groups of 30 stems or more. The individual stems are smaller than those of the claret cup hedgehog, less than 8 inches tall and 2 inches in diameter, with as many as 15 or 16 angular ribs. Its nearly spherical, brownish fruit is likely sought by beetles, rodents, and other animals who would disperse its seed with their scat. Almost certainly, ants collect the seeds and carry them off to new sites, as they are known to do with other hedgehogs. The large, brilliant pink flowers have dramatically splayed petals that can reach 5 inches in diameter and more than 4 inches tall, and as nectar producers they are probably a food source for hummingbirds and nectar-seeking insects.

This species grows at low elevations in semi-desert grasslands of the Sonoran Desert Region in east-central Sonora, Mexico, near the Río Yaqui and its northern tributaries, and in extreme southern Arizona. (The Arizona specimens are var. *pseudopectinatus*. Only one specimen of the Sonoran subspecies *Echinocereus bristolii bristolii* exists in Southwestern herbaria.) Some botanists think *E. bristolii* may be a variety of *E. scopulorum,* which grows on the west coast of Sonora, and/or *E. sciurus floresii*, which has much smaller flowers and grows in Sonora and Sinaloa. Little information is available on its status, but its limited distribution and small total population calls its viability into question given any significant natural or anthropogenic threat. Evidence from at least one study showed that a significant percent of hedgehog cactus have been killed by cattle trampling where grazing occurred in their habitat, so habitat use and conversion is likely a concern, as it is with many vulnerable grasslands species.

> THE WATER EFFICIENCY OF THE DESERT IRONWOOD TREE RANKS WITH SOME OF THE MOST DROUGHT TOLERANT SONORAN DESERT PLANTS.

DESERT IRONWOOD TREE
Olneya tesota

It is called "the desert tree of life." To wit, at least a few desert ironwood trees are thought to be 800 years old or more. Even in death it persists—an impenetrable, dense and weighty wood, lasting for another several hundred years, or a thousand; neither termites nor fungus nor bacterium, which usually break down dead plant materials, can tolerate the minerals in desert ironwood. *Palo fierro*, as it is known in Mexico, is so dense it will not float and is considered one of the "hardest and heaviest woods in the world," a metaphorical iron acknowledged by the common name in both its homeland languages.

However, the tree of life epithet refers more to the benefits it provides for hundreds of other species than to its longevity. Reaching heights of 35 feet or more, with trunks to 12 feet in diameter and 40-foot-wide canopies, this legume pulls from the soil and the sun to produce branches, leaves, flowers, and beans that provide essential resources to the animals and plants of Sonoran Desert communities. Like others in the legume family (Fabaceae), it bears bean pods containing seeds high in protein. These beans ripen as summer rains arrive, when little else is available to the creatures that eat them. Bees find pollen in its copious lavender flowers. Birds roost and nest on the branches, while the broad canopy brings the gift of shade for dozens of understory plants, protecting them from freezing or baking. Its decomposing leaf and pod litter helps provide nitrogen for the soil.

According to fossil records, desert ironwood was present in the early Holocene, perhaps 10,000 years ago, in what is now the Sonoran Desert Region. With the advance of a dry climate, this species adapted incredibly well. According to an Arizona-Sonora Desert Museum report, the water efficiency of this tree ranks with some of the most drought tolerant Sonoran Desert plants, such as creosotebush, bursage, and wolfberry. Desert ironwoods grow almost exclusively in the Sonoran Desert, from southern Arizona and southeastern California, south through much of the Baja California peninsula and in northwestern Sonora, Mexico. They are present in patches of thornscrub habitats near Guaymas and Hermosillo, Sonora. In the Arizona Upland, they thrive in porous soils on bajadas and low mountain slopes in an elevation band above cold drainages, where frost is minimized. In more arid habitats further south and west, they grow in washes and valley floors down to sea level.

In the late twentieth century, desert ironwood forests in Sonora, Mexico, were heavily harvested for charcoal and for commercial production of small sculptures, almost to the point of extirpation in many areas. In the United States, off-road vehicles are a concern. Conversion of ironwood habitat to agricultural or exurban land use also poses a threat, as does extended drought. Hot, unnatural fires sparked by introduced buffelgrass will also kill ironwood. Today, although *Olneya tesota* is not officially listed as threatened, it has legal protection in Sonora and Arizona. Even so, illegal harvests continue. Because it does not reproduce in great numbers and grows slowly, this species is particularly susceptible to illegal harvesting of trees.

IRONWOOD TREE
acrylic, 30" x 30"

WILLIAM HOOK

DESERT PEOPLE TRADITIONALLY FOUND SUSTENANCE IN THIS PLANT'S STARCHY TUBER.

DESERT NIGHT-BLOOMING CEREUS
Peniocereus greggii

If ever a cactus embodied a storyline, it is this one. In fact, cactus-lovers recognize *Peniocereus greggii* as the Cinderella of the Sonoran Desert. Most of the year, it is plain and unassuming, almost unsightly, camouflaged among a parched gray tangle of stems and branches where trees and shrubs offer shade and protection from trampling. But in the late spring, by some coincidence of planets and weather, its straggly ribbed stems slowly push out one or many 7-inch floral tubes. And on a given night in late May to mid-July, hundreds of *P. greggii* buds across scores of miles unfold their petals, unveiling a large, elegant cup of stamens. From petal tip to petal tip, this extravagant, stark white flower can be up to 4 inches across. It is no surprise that it is also called the "queen of the night" or *reina de la noche (*as well as *saramatraca)*.

Throughout the dark hours, this queen emits occasional bursts of ambrosial fragrance. The intoxicating scent (be warned, not all people can smell it) wafts through the desert scrub advertising its presence to the night-flying sphinx moths that pollinate this plant. In the early morning, bees and flies may also visit, but they are not efficient pollinators. At the first stroke of sun, the petals begin curling up into a ball. A large, bright red, fleshy fruit ripens a month later, offering nutritious pulp and seeds for birds and other desert creatures. Desert people traditionally found sustenance in this plant's starchy tuber, which looks like a giant turnip (possibly 10 inches by 15 inches).

Periodically the stems of *P. greggii* whither or are eaten by animals, but a new stem normally rises from the plump root in another season. Mature, healthy plants in the wild can have a dozen branches climbing 5 feet or so into a palo verde or mesquite tree, and they can easily flaunt two dozen flowers. Younger plants have few branches, but may still post several blossoms. Although most *P. greggii* buds across a broad landscape open on the same festive night, there are often two or more smaller flushes of bloom in a season.

Frost hardy and long-lived, the desert night-blooming cereus and its varieties are endemic to southern Arizona, southern New Mexico, western Texas, and Chihuahua, Zacatecas, and Sonora, Mexico. It lives in lowland flats, especially where creosote grows. *Peniocereus greggii* is now rare in New Mexico, Texas, and Mexico, in part due to collection for landscaping, but also because much of its habitat has been converted to urban or agricultural uses, including grazing. Populations of the Arizona queen of the night have declined, but not critically—yet. Unfortunately, in its natural habitat where agricultural fields are near, the use of pesticide can devastate populations of the hawk moths essential to the plants' survival, and conversion of its habitat continues. The desert night-blooming cereus is legally protected from collection in Arizona, but some nurseries and botanical institutions are producing seed-grown plants for collectors.

Rhonda Nass
Desert Night-blooming Cereus
acrylic, 8" x 10"

Kearny Sumac
Rhus kearneyi kearneyi

An attractive evergreen shrub, Kearny sumac has been around for longer than most species endemic to the region now called Arizona. Fossil evidence suggests that they are relics from the Tertiary Period, before the Pleistocene ice ages, when the Sierra Nevada range was still actively rising, when camels and horses still roamed through grasslands in North America, and well before *Homo sapiens* arrived in this continent.

Rhus kearneyi kearneyi can grow as a tree up to 13 feet high, but it is more often a large, broad shrub that grows on shaded east- or north-facing slopes, canyon walls, and drainages in desert scrub habitat. Its leathery green leaves grow densely on sturdy branches. They are veined with white, and can be lightly coated with a bluish down. Its red twigs and its fruit are also pubescent. (Some botanists speculate that pubescence on a fruit is a strategy to dissuade small insects and encourage birds and mammals to eat and disperse their seed.) From January through March, this sumac bears compact clusters of cream to pinkish flowers, and in the summer, hairy red oblong fruits to nearly a half-inch in length. Although the genus *Rhus* is probably best known for poison-ivy, -oak, and -sumac, not all *Rhus* are toxic. People use the berries of sugar sumac (*R. ovata*) to which *R. kearneyi* is closely related, for making a lemony beverage. And though not particularly tasty, berries of the Kearny sumac are also edible. These plants provide flowers, fruits, or cover for butterflies and birds.

Only a few populations of *R. kearnyi* are known; they grow sparsely in the Cabeza Prieta, Tinajas Altas, and Gila Mountains in southwestern Arizona—areas protected from development and heavy traffic by their remoteness or location on a military bombing range. In addition, domestic livestock do not eat the foliage of Kearny's sumac. Because its viability is threatened by its small numbers, however, and because it is an attractive shrub that might be appreciated in native landscaping, it has been grown out by botanical gardens for both exhibits and for potential use in commercial or private landscapes.

Only a few populations of Kearny sumac are known, all in southwestern Arizona.

DULCE NASCIMENTO
KEARNY SUMAC
watercolor, 20" x 12"

Kearney's Bluestar
Amsonia kearneyana

Kearny's bluestar is one of 18 species in the genus *Amsonia* growing in eastern Asia, Europe, and North America. It is one of five species of this genus found in the Four Corners area of the Southwest and in southwestern Arizona, Texas, and Sonora and Chihuahua, Mexico. Their direct ancestors are thought to have bloomed with the Earth's earliest flowering plants. Established in the American Southwest by the end of the Cretaceous Period, they adapted over thousands of years with climate fluctuations and an increasingly arid environment into distinct species in disparate locations. The five species of *Amsonia* found in the Southwest evolved stigmas with two lobes and narrow-mouthed blossoms, an adaptation that encourages pollination by insects in dry regions.

On a mature *Amsonia kearneyana*, dozens of fuzzy stems grow upright and close together to form an attractive, rounded shrub 2 or 3 feet high and as wide or wider, with long narrow leaves. In April or May, a small cluster of white and pale-blue blossoms grace the ends of the stems, the tip of each flower shaped like a star. (On some plants the flowers tend to pale pink.) Moths, possibly hawk moths, are considered likely pollinators for this shrub. Found only in northern Sonora (a population discovered in 1996) and in the Baboquivari Mountains of southern Arizona, populations of Kearny's bluestar are extremely limited, and shrinking. Following wet winters, the seeds of this and a nearby, closely-related *Amsonia* species have been plagued with stinkbugs that eviscerate the seed, preventing successful reproduction almost entirely. In dry years fewer beetles attack, and most seeds remain fertile. Fruits develop between June and August.

Kearny's bluestar grows in rocky washes and on open slopes of canyons at 3,600 to 6,000 feet in desert scrub or semi-desert grassland habitat, along with Mexican blue oak, velvet mesquite, hackberry, cat claw acacia, Arizona walnut, and desert cotton. In 1986, only 8 Kearny's bluestar plants were known from Arizona, and only from one canyon in the Baboquivaris. Since then, several other plants have been found, but the total population of *A. kearneyana* remains extremely small. Under a critical habitat program for federally endangered species, as well as private seed-collection and cultivation programs, more than 200 plants were reintroduced in the Baboquivaris in the late 1980s. (Some of those plants were grown out at the Arizona-Sonora Desert Museum.) But with flooding, insect damage, and habitat disturbance or direct trampling by grazing animals, more than half those transplants did not survive. The Sonoran population is also very small. In an effort to save the species from extinction, seeds are being grown out in botanical institutions for potential use in residential landscapes, and wild seeds are being banked for future restoration efforts.

KEARNY'S BLUESTAR IS FOUND ONLY IN NORTHERN SONORA, MEXICO, AND IN SOUTHERN ARIZONA.

MANABU C. SAITO
KEARNY'S BLUESTAR
watercolor, 17" x 15"

> TODAY, NICHOL'S TURK'S HEAD CACTUS ARE KNOWN FROM ONLY FOUR LOCATIONS, AND THESE POPULATIONS ARE THOUGHT TO INCLUDE FEWER THAN 5,000 PLANTS ALTOGETHER.

NICHOL'S TURK'S HEAD CACTUS
Echinocactus horizonthalonius var. *nicholii*

In the Sonoran Desert's dramatic cactus opera, the bloom of the Nichol's Turk's head is a diva. Its petals flash seductively in a dazzling, iridescent pink or deep fuchsia, with a basal band of rich, glowing red. Large and showy, up to 3 inches in diameter, these luminaries invite, and satisfy, their audience. In fact, bees dive in and out of its dense forest of delicate golden stamens with seeming intoxicated frenzy. With pollination services properly rendered, a vivid pink fruit develops concealed under a tuft of white fuzz. When ripe, the fruit will split and trickle the bulk of its seed to the ground. The fluffy tuft dries and persists until another bud rises through it, pushing out the remaining seeds. As if for our viewing pleasure, the Nichol's Turk's head cactus blooms not once but several times, from April to July and often with rains in late summer or early fall; however, the flowers are fully open for only a few hours at midday in peak sunlight. This perennial succulent grows as a single blue-green to gray-green stem up to 20 inches high with eight ribs that, in older plants, typically spiral from the base to the top. Very slow growing, it takes a dozen years or more to reach an inch diameter.

Echinocactus horizonthalonius var. *nicholii* is almost always found in soils derived from limestone. Fossils in packrat middens show that it has been growing in the same localities for more than 22,000 years, before its habitat became Sonoran Desert. Today, only four known locations hold Nichol's Turk's head cactus—the Waterman Mountains, Koht Kohl Hills, and Vekol Mountains in southern Arizona, and the Sierra El Viejo in Sonora, Mexico. These populations are thought to include fewer than 5,000 plants altogether, and the surveyed populations are declining. The Sierra El Viejo population lies in an area recently set aside for protection, and a portion of the Waterman Mountains falls into the recently designated Ironwood Forest National Monument, but enforcement of legal protections in these locations remains difficult. At one time, mining operations were the major threat to this species, but since the late twentieth century trampling by off-road vehicles and cactus thievery has been of more concern. In addition, the bane of introduced buffelgrass now plagues the Waterman Mountains landscape, building fuels for hot fires destructive to Sonoran Desert communities. While conservation groups and government agencies are eradicating buffelgrass and have succeeded in clearing undisturbed areas of the Watermans, this invasive grass spreads rapidly, and rigorous sustained effort will likely be required to keep it under control.

Nichol's Turk's Head Cactus
watercolor, 12" x 15.5"

Lívia Vieira

WILLIAM HOOK
"ORGAN PIPE"
acrylic, 30" x 30"

ORGAN PIPE CACTUS
Stenocereus thurberi

This sun-loving, succulent candelabra moved into what is now the Sonoran Desert from more tropical habitats of Mexico about 3,500 years ago. The organ pipe cactus has waterproof skin that inhibits the loss of moisture, and unlike saguaro, the seedlings don't need shade from a tree or shrub to thrive under the hot sun. As it matures, this cactus grows more stems (up to 24 or more) that are typically about 8 inches in diameter and 10 feet tall, although they are sometimes twice that height. The multiple stems of this columnar cactus capitalize on the increased green surface to capture more sun and thus increase production of chlorophyll for energy. This cactus is susceptible to frost, and repeated annular constrictions (indentations) on its stems show that the stem tips have frozen back at intervals in its life. An organ pipe cactus won't flower for the first 35 years or so, waiting until it reaches 6 to 8 feet in height and has four or more limbs. After that, it blooms each May and June, producing dozens of blossoms every remaining year of its potential 150-year lifespan.

The pale pink or white flowers of *Stenocereus thurberi* open at night and usually close by mid-morning, well after the night-flying lesser long-nosed bats have tracked its musky floral smell to glean their pollen. The red fruits, bigger than a ping pong ball, are ready to eat at the hottest, driest part of the year, before the summer rains begin, and are relished by birds, rodents, wasps, and other desert creatures, including the thousands of female bats that roost with their babies in Organ Pipe Cactus National Monument each summer. The fruits are sweet, and are widely regarded to be one of the most delicious cactus fruits (the cactus is called *pitaya dulce* in Mexico). Native American people have long eaten these wild treats. The Seri people used the woody core of *pitaya dulce* for building material and used the pulp as an ingredient in sealant for their boats.

Also known as *mehuele* and *organo marismeña* in Mexico, *S. thuberi* is found along the Sonoran coast, in the lower half of the Baja peninsula, and just inside Sinaloa and Chihuahua. It is most abundant in thornscrub and tropical deciduous forest habitats of Sonora, where the branches grow off the stem from a height of 6 feet or more, nearer the level of the surrounding tree canopy (a strategy that helps them capture more sunlight). Organ pipe barely reaches into the United States, where it flourishes on south-facing slopes in Organ Pipe Cactus National Monument, just north of the international border, and in nearby areas such as the Tohono O'odham Nation. In Arizona, the organ pipe cactus is afforded protection and lies largely in protected areas, but in Mexico the familiar storm of habitat conversion for agricultural use and aquaculture has become a serious threat.

> ALTHOUGH ITS TOTAL RANGE MAY COVER UP TO 600 SQUARE MILES, RESEARCHERS ESTIMATE WITHIN THAT EXPANSE ONLY ABOUT 20 POPULATIONS EXIST, AND INDIVIDUAL PIMA PINEAPPLE CACTI ARE ONLY LIGHTLY PEPPERED ON THOSE LANDS.

Pima Pineapple Cactus
Coryphantha robustispina

The rare Pima pineapple cactus protects its moist interior flesh from thirsty denizens of the desert with a network of thick spines—10 to 15 pale-ochre or age-darkened spines radiating around a central spine at the end of each knobby protrusion of its stem. (Young plants usually have no central and only 6 radial spines.) The most robust, mature plants can reach 8 inches in diameter and 18 inches tall, but most are more modest, with an oval or rounded profile for the single stem; they may also grow in clusters of several stems. Through winter and spring, its only ornament is its spiny armor, but with the onset of monsoon rains, one to several buds emerge to unfold delicate pale yellow flowers on its crown. In the fall, with successful pollination, a green juicy fruit matures into a sweet treat that will quench dry throats and nourish arid-land animals.

Also known as "Scheer's strong-spined cory cactus," *Coryphantha robustispina* thrives in alluvial soils on flat open terrain or on bajadas at lower elevations in semi-desert grassland and Sonoran Desert scrub from southern Arizona, south of Tucson, to northern Sonora, Mexico, including a large swath of the Tohono O'odham Nation. Although its total range may cover up to 600 square miles, within that expanse, researchers estimate only about 20 populations exist, and individual Pima pineapple cacti are only lightly peppered on those lands. Forty percent or more of its known historical habitat has already been given over to urban or exurban development or mining, or it has been degraded by overgrazing or off-road vehicles. Invasion of nonnative grasses like Lehmann's lovegrass and other exotic vegetation hampers the emergence of new plants and produces fuel for wildfire, to which the Pima pineapple cactus, like most Sonoran Desert species, is not adapted and does not survive. Finally, illegal collection for the horticultural trade has diminished its populations.

In Arizona, the rapid decline of this little succulent helped inspire the Pima County Sonoran Desert Conservation Plan in southern Arizona, which protects open lands to benefit *C. robustispina* and all the rooted and mobile creatures in those habitats. It was listed as an endangered species in the United States in 1993. A few horticultural institutions cultivate the Pima pineapple cactus, including the Arizona-Sonora Desert Museum. To better understand the needs and relationships of this species within its natural community, the Museum has also conducted research on its pollination dynamics, growth rate, seed dispersal, and predation.

Joan McGann
Pima Pineapple Cactus
colored pencil, 27" x 18"

In Arizona, the rapid decline of this little succulent helped inspire Pima County's Sonoran Desert Conservation Plan— a plan that protects open lands to benefit the Pima Pineapple cactus and all the rooted and mobile creatures in those habitats.

Pima Pineapple Cactus Flower
acrylic, 10" x 8"

Rhonda Nass

PIMA PINEAPPLE CACTUS FRUIT
acrylic, 10" x 8"

RHONDA NASS

A FEW HORTICULTURAL INSTITUTIONS CULTIVATE THE PIMA PINEAPPLE CACTUS, INCLUDING THE ARIZONA-SONORA DESERT MUSEUM.

TWO SUBSPECIES OF *MAMMILLARIA SABOAE* ARE ENDEMIC TO SONORA, MEXICO.

SABO'S PINCUSHION CACTUS
Mammillaria saboae

Of all the Mammillarias—a very large genus of very small cacti—Sabo's pincushion has the smallest stems and one of the largest flowers. In fact, the flowers are significantly larger than the stem itself. The globular or ovoid stems of this tiny cactus only grow to 1½ inches high and wide, with one of the three subspecies somewhat smaller. Unless they are in flower, they easily go unnoticed. They can grow as a single stem or in clumps, but each head of the Sabo's pincushion has a neat, round, geometric form, its flesh symmetrically studded with miniature hillocks. In two of the subspecies, *saboae* (the nominate subspecies) and *haudeana*, each tiny green mound is topped by 17 to 27 shiny, delicate white spines radiating from the aureole like the tentacles of tiny sea anemones, while the *goldii* subspecies has 34 to 45 radial spines.

About 2½ inches long and slightly more in diameter, the bright pink petals splay open at the end of a narrow throat, with the pink paling toward the center of the blossom. In spring, a clump of this cactus might bear a single flower or several flowers blooming in quick succession, but they are not arranged in the ring pattern often associated with *Mammillaria*. In another wayward adaptation for its genus, the fruit of Sabo's pincushion doesn't protrude, but actually matures sunken into the flesh of the stem, showing up only as a rusty scar on the green skin.

Two subspecies of *Mammillaria saboae* are endemic to Sonora, Mexico. *Mammillaria saboae goldii*, which typically grows as a single stem, is only known from two places in northwestern Sonora, near Nacozari—one a mountain habitat, the other a valley. *Mammillaria saboae haudeana*—the larger form, but still diminutive at about 1½ inches high—typically clumps. It grows in poor, often bare, soils in the Sierra Madre Occidental, near Yecora, and is locally abundant. Although the small range and limited populations of Sabo's pincushion cactus make it vulnerable to local assaults, natural or anthropogenic, all three subspecies are cultivated and usually available commercially. In cultivation, the clumps can be large and tight, and the flowers profuse.

SABO'S PINCUSHION CACTUS   BOBBIE BROWN
watercolor, 10.5" x 9"

> BECAUSE ITS DISTRIBUTION IS SO LIMITED,
> THE SURVIVAL OF *ECHINOCEREUS LEUCANTHUS*
> IS VULNERABLE TO INCREASING CONVERSION OF
> THORNSCRUB TO AGRICULTURAL USES.

SLENDER CLIMBING CACTUS
Echinocereus leucanthus

Small, elegant flowers grace the slender stems of *Echinocereus leucanthus*. By some accounts, the botanist who first recorded the species in 1952 kept the location of this little spined jewel to himself for a decade or so. But when a population of the slender climbing cactus was rediscovered in the 1960s, horticulturalists lost no time raising it in their nurseries for cactus aficionados (who never bothered to assign it a common name until the twenty-first century, although its scientific name changed from *Wilcoxia albiflora* to *Echinocereus leucanthus*). The genus *Echinocereus* comprises approximately 70 species, with about 40 subspecies. Most of these species are clumping cactus with thick cylindrical or globular stems and are known as hedgehogs, but a few, like this slender climbing cactus, are long and spindly.

Like the desert night-blooming cereus, this small plant is hard to find unless it is blooming. Its plump, tuberous root sends up green to purple-green stems that climb and branch to a foot or more high, typically supported by growing through shrubs such as the California boxthorn. Fine spines radiate from tiny, closely packed, woolly bumps on the ridge of its ribs, a classic cactus strategy for protecting its flesh from herbivores. In the summer, white or light pink flowers appear, funnel-shaped and tapering to a brownish base, typically at the apex or occasionally off the side of the upper stem. The blossoms stay open for several days, closing at night and reopening the following morning, so pollinators are likely to be crepuscular or diurnal insects. Two months after pollination, a sweet-smelling, dark green, fleshy fruit ripens.

The slender climbing cactus grows sparsely in hot coastal thornscrub at low elevations, near Guaymas in southwestern Sonora and near Los Mochis in northwestern Sinaloa. It is registered as a rare endemic by the Mexican government. Because its distribution is so limited, the survival of *E. leucanthus* is vulnerable to increasing conversion of thornscrub to agricultural uses.

Rhonda Nass
Slender Climbing Cactus
colored pencil, 9" x 16"

Altar Valley, Southern Arizona

When monsoon rain sweeps the oaks and pines in southern Arizona's Baboquivari Mountains, waters gather and race downhill. On an eastern slope of the range, they race toward the Altar Wash, where they join the waters of other slopes flowing north through the Buenos Aires National Wildlife Refuge and on through most of the 50-mile length of the Altar Valley. In the refuge, a ciénega, a creek, and semi-desert grassland invite the flutter, soar, trills, screams, and warbles of thousands of birds, as well as the measured step of four-legged browsers and hunters. In fact, most of the avian species and several of the plants and animals portrayed in the Vanishing Circles collection lived in, live in, or visit the Altar Valley.

Not a century ago, the aplomado falcon found forage and nesting in a lush grassland here. Today, coveys of masked bobwhite quail still forage and nest there due to long-term reintroduction and management efforts. Though significantly diminished, the grasses and dense riparian vegetation also host Bell's vireos, Abert's towhees, rufous-winged sparrows, yellow-billed cuckoos, and violet-crowned hummingbirds (not to mention ten other hummingbird species), as well as the not-so-rare but blazingly beautiful lazuli buntings, vermilion flycatchers, tanagers, orioles, and even an occasional elegant trogon, least tern, or wayward crested caracara or brown pelican! In more arid locations of the valley and mountain slopes, cactus ferruginous pygmy owls find a home, mountain lions stalk deer, and bears dream of honey. In Brown Canyon, near a small stream in an oak woodland of the Baboquivaris, the roots of the rare Kearny's bluestar draw from the soil to fuel their blooms.

Although human feet have tread the basin and hills of the Altar Valley for more than 10,000 years, and in spite of grasslands depauperated in the last century by intense grazing and since invaded by mesquite and other shrubby growth, the valley is still largely open, still wild, still harboring nests, burrows, and calving grounds for more than 55 species of mammals and more than 50 species of reptiles or amphibians. Even the elusive jaguar has been tracked here. In fact, the Altar Valley harbors about two dozen species of plants or animals of special concern. Its varied landscapes are bound on the west by the Coyote, Quinlan, and Baboquivari Mountains; the Cerro Colorado Mountains rise on the east central flank, with the Buenos Aires National Wildlife Refuge and Forest Service land to the west and south as far as the Mexican-American border.

In the early 1800s, lush native bunch grasses growing across most of the valley supported healthy populations of grassland species. Great herds of pronghorn raced here. But by the late nineteenth century heavy cattle grazing, mining, and water diversions had irreversibly altered the grasslands. Native grasses were displaced by the invasive Lehmann lovegrass (introduced for fodder); and fires, which once swept the valley regularly, were suppressed, allowing mesquite and other shrubs to encroach on open spaces. Finally, in 1985, the U.S. Fish and Wildlife Service bought the 118,000-acre Buenos Aires Ranch, establishing the wildlife refuge and reintroduction programs for both masked bobwhite and American pronghorn. On the refuge, efforts to eradicate Lehmann lovegrass are ongoing, and old ranch fencing is being removed. Ranchers in other parts of the Altar Valley, where desert scrub dominates, are working to control erosion brought about by historic overgrazing of native grasses, and have also created a "bank" for the endangered Pima pineapple cactus.

John N. Agnew
"Waiting for Rain"
acrylic, 20" x 30"

Aravaipa Canyon, Arizona

A seamless meld of stunning beauty and ecological treasure, Aravaipa Canyon evokes reflections on pristine wilderness centuries past. Through this canyon, perennial waters flow east to west seeking the San Pedro River. These cool currents harbor seven species of desert fish, including the rare loach minnow and spikedace. While nonnative fish have found their way here, their numbers are still mercifully low, and the creek is one of the healthiest native fisheries in Arizona. On either side of the creek, rock walls rise 1,000 feet—beyond them, rough, thorny tablelands. Saguaros dot the slopes and cliffs, while thick-trunked Arizona walnut, cottonwood, and sycamore raise a vibrant green canopy in the bottomlands each spring. Here, warm-weather hikers may stumble upon a slender snake in a slate blue topcoat with a thin orange necklace and a bright yellow belly grading to pure vermilion under the tail—a snake aptly called the regal ringneck snake. Western ornate box turtles trundle along the creek, while bighorn sheep maneuver across the canyon's rocky ledges and coatimundi troop from hillside to shady grove. Brilliant red zauschneria and cardinal flowers attract hummingbirds, while queen butterflies swarm to masses of yellow composites in the fall. In side canyons, lacey ferns and monkeyflowers carpet broad patches where seeps ooze darkly over steep, pitted walls.

More than 150 species of songbirds nest or visit here, including rare yellow-billed cuckoos and southwestern willow flycatchers. In warm seasons, day winds carry black hawks and gray hawks, while belted kingfishers wing overhead in the fall, and ferruginous hawks fly in winter. At night, the call of western screech owls can be heard, as well as leopard frogs in season. Mountain lion, black bear, deer, and other animals drop down to the creek for water. Aravaipa canyonland is, indeed, a rich natural landscape, but not so rich as it once was.

When settlers from the East first arrived, beavers still dammed the stream, creating backwater pools and slowing the river's flow, which helped to keep the water table high. Grizzly bears were already gone, but gray wolves and prairie dogs persisted. Today, all of these have been extirpated. While the rugged terrain of the canyon and surrounding uplands kept the trappings of civilization out of the inner canyon, miners turned up on its periphery in the late 1800s, and ranchers and farmers moved onto the lush bottomlands at both ends. Residents and visitors of all stripes hunted game, including Apaches, who also harvested wild foods. By the mid 1900s, the local mining industry had come and gone, leaving toxic tailings behind. And everyone had cut heavily into the forests and streambanks for fuel and field clearings. In fact, professional woodcutters downed truckloads of huge walnuts and sycamores for the furniture industry. By the 1970s nonnative trees such as salt cedar had reached the canyon, joining Russian thistle, red brome, and other exotic plants.

In 1984, the U.S. government recognized the natural value of Aravaipa Canyon with the designation of the 11-mile canyon as federal Wilderness. With additions made in 1990, the Wilderness Area now includes nine side canyons and nearly 20,000 surrounding acres. The Bureau of Land Management manages this Wilderness Area, while The Nature Conservancy and private landowners hold the land at either end.

KEN STOCKTON
ARAVAIPA CANYON
oil, 18" x 24"

Gran Desierto de Altar, U.S.-Mexico Borderland

In this land of little rain, dunes crawl across the Earth, shapeshifting with the winds into pyramidal stars with "arms," concave crescents, and straight or winding ridges. The highest dunes crest at almost 600 feet above the trough. The sand blows low, sweeping and building against solitary forms, its sheer power dictating habits to the plants and wildlife that live and evolve in this grainy sea. The Algodones Dunes (some 240 square miles in southeastern California and northeastern Baja California) are the northernmost reach of the Gran Desierto de Altar—4,800 square miles of active sand dunes that lie mostly in northwestern Sonora, Mexico. The Gran Desierto is the largest active, or moving, sand sea in North America. The lion's share of the incalculable sand grains in these dunes eroded over a few million years from rock in the Grand Canyon, swept by the Colorado River either to the Pleistocene Lake Cahuilla (when the river wavered to the west), or to the delta in the Gulf of California.

In spite of a measly few inches of rain each year and summer temperatures often above 110 degrees Fahrenheit, the sand hills of the Gran Desierto harbor at least 85 species of plants, dozens of species of vertebrates, and hundreds of species of invertebrates. Many of the plants here, including creosotebush, grow tall rather than wide, a trait thought to mitigate the effects of blowing and drifting sands and also prevent burial. They drive their roots downward to capture deep-percolating water. The rare Peirson's milk-vetch can push its taproot down 4 feet, while its fuzzy leaves help prevent sunburn and minimize evapotranspiration. Another endemic denizen is the parasitic "sand food," an edible plant whose tuberous roots were traditionally enjoyed by Native Americans. After relatively generous winter and spring rains, this severe landscape clamors with wildflowers like pink sand verbena, white-blossomed dune evening primrose, and spectacle-pod. Whatever grows on the dunes or along the hardpan drainages provides fodder for scarab and buprestid beetles, bees, weevils, ants, and such, which become prey for larger dune dwellers, like the Sonoran Desert fringe-toed lizard, a speedy runner and skilled burrower that can dive into and "swim" through the sand. The shovel-nosed sand snake also swims the sands. Kit foxes, kangaroo rats, pocket mice, and other small quadrupeds make tracks on the surface.

For thousands of years, Native American tribes lived in and traveled through the Algodones Dunes and the Gran Desierto. They left artifacts, but little environmental damage. The twentieth century brought more significant impacts. In the name of progress, men constructed State Highway 78 and the "All American" Canal (which only serves the United States) through the Algodones Dunes. This place also became a recreational haven, with jeeps and dune buggies swarming its mounds. (It was once dubbed the "national desecration area" by biologist-author Frederich Gehlbach, who described "mauled shrubs and mashed creatures" in his *History of the U. S. Borderlands* of 1981—before the number of visitors to the Algodones Dunes tripled between 1985 and 2001.) In addition, flood control projects, power lines, mining ventures, and illegal foot traffic have degraded the dunes. In 1994, the government set aside 30,000 acres in the Algodones Dunes as a National Wilderness Area, but more than 80 percent of the Algodones Dunes are still open to abuse. State Highway 78, shown in the painting, borders the south side of the Wilderness Area. To the north, vegetation is evident; to the south, where off-road vehicle traffic is allowed, the dunes are barren. Luckily, the Mexican portion of the Gran Desierto has seen far less human or vehicular traffic; it is part of a United Nations-designated Biosphere Reserve, the Pinacate and Gran Desierto de Altar Biosphere Reserve.

"Line in the Sand" - Algodone Dunes
acrylic, 24" x 24"

William Hook

KEN STOCKTON
SABINO CANYON
oil, 23" x 31"

SABINO CANYON, SOUTHERN ARIZONA

On the southern face of the Santa Catalina Mountains, a sparkling creek edged with lush, leafy deciduous trees runs through the rocky cliffs of Sabino Canyon. It is a stunning, refreshing sanctuary that attracts a million visitors a year, tourists and local residents alike. Here, cool waters spill over giant boulders polished by centuries of floods. Bordered with cottonwood, willow, sycamore, ash, and walnut trees, this stream descends thousands of feet between rock walls and steep slopes barbed with giant saguaros and sharply bladed agaves and yuccas. This thorny high ground is Sonoran Desert scrub, heavy with palo verde and other drought-tolerant plants. Beyond the scrub, shrubs like turpentine bush, oreganillo, and ocotillo punctuate semi-desert grassland; further upslope is Madrean evergreen woodland, where fir, pine, juniper, and oak dominate the landscape. It is a mix of natural communities that fosters rampant biodiversity.

In small pools along the creek, snails, tadpoles, and insect larvae eat algae from the rocks while larger insects, snakes, lizards, and other animals hunt these creatures for prey. From dusk to dawn, when people are few or absent, white-tailed deer, javelina, bobcat, raccoon, ringtail, and other mammals make their way to the creek for water, while canyon bats, like the little western pipistrelles, swoop to its surface to drink. At night, great horned owls hoot. In the day, red-tailed hawks scout prey, and small birds rest or nest in leafy branches, some of them dashing out to pluck airborne insects. In winter, belted kingfishers fish the creek. These are just a few of the evident natural wonders. But this canyon also holds less obvious wonders—some as obscure as they are delightful—like the tiny freshwater "jellyfish." Up to one inch across, this gelatinous tentacled creature looks for all the world like a miniature oceanic jellyfish pulsing through the water. Last reported here about two decades ago, it is actually a life stage of a nonnative colonial polyp that lives on rocks underwater.

Sabino Creek is fed by precipitation in the mountains, whence rain and snowmelt moves downhill, mainly below ground, surfacing as it funnels through the canyon. In winter the creek swells, while in the parched months before and after summer monsoons, it trickles then dries up, leaving only small pools to refresh the wildlife and bridge the drought for aquatic life. (It is in these dry periods that the medusoid form of the polyp is seen.) In the monsoon season, flash floods carry debris from above into the lower canyon, enriching its soils.

Since the time of the Clovis culture some 13,000 years ago, people have made use of the canyon's resources. In the late nineteenth century, with nearby Tucson burgeoning, it became a favored destination, a place to picnic and swim, and in 1902, the "Arizona Forest Reserve" was set aside by Congress, including Sabino Canyon. More than once, upper Sabino Canyon was targeted for a dam and water reservoir; luckily, that ambition was thwarted by a well-timed drought. During the Great Depression, various public works programs sponsored the building of a road (now closed to vehicles) and bridges. Inevitably, with the people, came the exotic plants and animals. Although Gila chub still swim in the upper canyon, Gila topminnow disappeared after the creek was stocked with mosquitofish and crayfish. Bermuda grass, red brome, and other invasives are now common in the canyon, while widespread nonnative fountaingrass creates fuel for destructive wildfires. The introduction of alien species is now prohibited, but curtailing established invasives here is already practically impossible.

ALREADY, 10 OF 14 NATIVE FISH THAT WRIGGLED THROUGH ITS WATERS NOT LONG AGO ARE GONE OR VIRTUALLY GONE FROM THE SAN PEDRO RIVER.

SAN PEDRO RIVER, ARIZONA

The fresh water and green corridor of the San Pedro River tender a profusion of life. From Sonora, Mexico, its headwaters gather and flow north across the border, passing the Huachuca Mountains, and finally spilling, undammed, into the Gila River southeast of Phoenix, Arizona. Although most of southern Arizona's rivers are rivers in name only (flowing only after rains except in short stretches), on its more than 100-mile course nearly 40 per cent of the San Pedro River is perennial, its clear waters flowing year round. Mixed stands of Fremont cottonwood and Goodding willow, North America's rarest forest type, still tower over the river. This riparian corridor supports about 100 breeding and 250 migrant birds that forage in the forest and surrounding scrub—among them, the elusive gray hawk, green kingfisher, and northern beardless-tyrannulet. For Neotropical migrating birds, the San Pedro is a major, and critical, highway. But it isn't just birds. Some 80 mammal species, 40 reptile and amphibian species, and dozens of species of butterflies find cover and food in and along the San Pedro. Bobcats and mountain lion hunt and drink here; even ocelot slip along its banks on rare occasions. Mule and white-tailed deer are relatively abundant, as are the Sonoran box turtle and lowland leopard frog. Here and there along its skirts, the increasingly rare sacaton grass grows lush.

And yet, the current flow of the San Pedro is marginal. Already, 12 of 14 native fish that wriggled through its waters not long ago are gone or virtually gone. Only the longfin dace and desert sucker remain in number. Instead, invasive yellow bullheads, common carp, and mosquitofish dominate the stream. Although hundreds of beaver worked the San Pedro two centuries ago, creating countless ponds and ciénegas that recharged the groundwater, by the mid-twentieth century they had been extirpated, indirectly, by deforestation, and directly. The Mexican spotted owl now hovers on the verge of extirpation here.

continued

"Riparian Respite"
oil, 19.5" x 23.5"

Les Lull

THE FREEFLOWING, LIFE-GIVING SAN PEDRO RIVER MAY SOON BE AN INTERMITTENT WASH, MOSTLY DRY, WITH IMPOVERISHED OR NO GREEN CORRIDOR, LIKE THE SANTA CRUZ.

SAN PEDRO RIVER, ARIZONA *continued*

Along the river, the semi-desert grasslands and Sonoran Desert uplands have long been cattle country. Ranchers from Mexico first came into the San Pedro Valley in the early nineteenth century. By the mid-nineteenth century, settlers from the East arrived to farm and ranch; later, Fort Huachuca attracted more residents. Finally, in 1988, the U.S. Congress created the San Pedro Riparian National Conservation Area along the southern 40 miles of the river in the United States. However, with continually increasing human populations and concomitant groundwater pumping (primarily for Sierra Vista and Fort Huachuca), land protection will not be enough. The freeflowing, life-giving San Pedro River may soon be an intermittent wash, mostly dry, with impoverished or no green corridor, like the Santa Cruz.

Since the 1940s, the quantity of water in the San Pedro has been reduced by about 65 percent. Although a long list of civic, military, and conservation groups, and a multitude of concerned individuals have been working together toward sustaining and restoring surface flow over the last two decades, projections for future flows based on current groundwater pumping are sobering. Broadbased and intense water conservation will be critical. But other approaches are also being taken. In an effort to slow its waters to increase surface flow and groundwater recharge, the Bureau of Land Management reintroduced 16 beavers between 1999 and 2003, and by 2008, 80 beavers were successfully working the river.

SAN PEDRO RIVER
oil, 12" x 16"

SHARI JONES

> RESIDENTIAL AND COMMERCIAL DEVELOPMENT ALONG THE COAST HAS KNOCKED THE WILD BREATH OUT OF ONCE PLENTIFUL AND HEALTHY ESTUARIES AND *ESTEROS*, PLACES THAT SERVED AS HOME OR CRITICAL NURSERIES FOR FISH AND SHELLFISH, BIRDS, AND CROCODILES.

Sea of Cortez, Mexico

The Sea of Cortez (also known as the Gulf of California) is the stage of unusual magic, a place that tugs at some ancient knowledge within us—a place of sun and flashing light and reckless spray, the home of slick-skinned bodies of a thousand shapes, from forage fish to finned or "winged" leviathans. It is a shoal of sardines, a speed of sharks, a smack of jellyfish, and oozes of slimy amorphous invertebrates in and outside of shells. It is crabs and sunstars. It is giant squid and the sperm whale that drive them to slaughter in the deep; it is a swordfish leaping high out of its dense blue domicile, spinning and crashing back through its roof. It is the heavy-winged flight of pelicans, the dive of brown boobies, and the cry of terns. It is the tenacious will of the horn shark. Barnacles. Plankton. It is a maelstrom of life.

For the bean counters among us, the surface of the Sea of Cortez encompasses more than 100,000 watery square miles between the Baja peninsula and mainland Mexico. It holds 5,000 named marine invertebrates (and easily that many more still awaiting names and descriptions), nearly 1,000 fish species, 34 marine mammals, and 5 sea turtles—altogether, about 6,000 species that have been identified and can be seen by the naked eye (not including plankton). Of seaweeds alone, or macroalgae, there are about 600 species. Five to six million years ago, shifting tectonic plates formed the Baja California peninsula and some 900 captured islands and islets. On these islands and along the coast, *esteros* and estuaries, beaches, and boulders support a menagerie of terrestial and avian animals, many of them endemic, including reptiles, mammals, and hundreds of bird species. A tiny fish lives in the anus of a sea cucumber; pelicans nest in mangroves or skim the waves to harvest oily detritus left by porpoise. Bats have taken up the practice of fishing. They are all connected.

continued

"Mangrove Bay"
acrylic, 24" x 24"

WILLIAM HOOK

> ONCE ABUNDANT IN THE SEA OF CORTEZ, EVERY SPECIES OF PREDATORY FISH IS NOW RARE.

SEA OF CORTEZ *continued*

However, this great abundance has brought droves of fishermen and a commercial industry. Bottom-trawling equipment on shrimp boats have wiped out entire sea-bottom communities and incidentally kills tons of other marine animals every year. Gill nets and long lines also cause inordinate destruction. Another, often unnoticed, threat to the aquatic ecosystem is the collecting of marine life by residents and tourists. Residential and commercial development along the coast have knocked the wild breath out of once plentiful and healthy estuaries and *esteros*, places that served as home or critical nurseries for fish and shellfish, birds, and crocodiles.

Once abundant here, every species of predatory fish is now rare. The totoaba, which was commercially fished until Mexico banned its harvest in 1975, is still in trouble. All the sharks are disappearing. In fact, populations of sharks and sea turtles here are now estimated at about 10 percent of their historic numbers. Corvina, stingrays, and the giant brown sea cucumber are also sliding off the sonar. One endemic, the vaquita, a rare small porpoise, has long been the victim of "incidental" deaths in commercial fishing nets and is now critically endangered.

In recent years, conservation organizations have been pushing for protected areas, effective laws, and less destructive fishing methods. In 1964, the first protected area in the Gulf, Isla Rasa, was established to protect the rare elegant tern. Since 1990 or so, a growing conservation movement in northwestern Mexico has attracted world attention (and international dollars), and today the Sea of Cortez is one of the best-protected large marine ecosystems in the world. With this protection, the fisheries should recover and the great predators will hopefully return to this wild oceanic region.

"Tropic of Cancer"
acrylic, 24" x 24"

WILLIAM HOOK

Tropical Deciduous Forest, Sonora, Mexico

Where wet and dry seasons two-step across the year; where thickly set, flower-laden bean trees cohabit with spiny, succulent pillars; where vines and epiphytes hug rugose, smooth-barked, or thorny trunks; and where bulbous, twisting roots cache water for many waxing moons—where all of this comes together, there you will find a dry tropical forest, also called "tropical deciduous forest." In the Oligocene Epoch, tropical forests covered much of North America, but as the climate dried over eons, they receded. Now only dry tropical forests flourish and only along the west coast of southwestern Sonora, Mexico, and on through Sinaloa to Panama and South America. Here, in this narrow strip of land, distinctive arboreal and floral forms abound: the deep fluting of the Brasil tree, the graceful petals of cuajilote, the feathery green foliage of tepeguaje, the conical thorns studding the lofty kapok tree—a tree whose seed-pod fluff has stuffed countless pillows over the centuries. The tropical deciduous forest in Mexico is considered one of the most biodiverse dry tropical forests on Earth, and also one of the rarest.

Near the old colonial town of Alamos in southern Sonora, one of the largest remaining tracts of tropical deciduous forest in the New World still thrives. In this place, an estimated 5,000 plant species, including 300 tree species, present an intricate tapestry of shapes and colors. Legumes dominate this dense forest, with seven species of columnar cactuses growing among them. Succulent shrubs and trees with contorted or swollen bases, like elephant trees and rock figs, are common. In fact, it is said that the tropical deciduous forest is so rich in succulent and semi-succulent trees that it cannot carry fire during the dry season. And unlike in temperate forests, blossoms emerge on one plant or another virtually all year. Some flower in the dry, leafless seasons, while others respond to the rainy seasons, and some with any rain, which makes for a constantly changing landscape in a land where winter and summer bring a total of about 30 inches of rain annually—nearly all, summer rain. The pink-trumpet tree and coral bean tree bear colorful blossoms in the gray or red-brown, bare-boned forest. Other species flower with pervasive new-sprung foliage. Each contributes in some way to the natural community. The tree morning glory produces showy white flowers that the Sinaloan whitetail deer like to eat; deer also trim the foliage of the guayacan tree, while birds eat the seeds of its fruit.

In the Alamos area, the forest is bisected by the fabled Río Cuchujaqui, whose green banks are lined with Montezuma bald cypress trees reaching 100 feet into the air, their branches alive with brilliantly feathered motmots, macaws, rare crane hawks, and other tropical wonders. Other animals hunting prey or harvesting edibles in this forest are the powerful jaguar and rare margay, the large and outspoken black-throated magpie jay, the lilac-crowned parrot, the nine-banded armadillo, the indigo snake, the "horrible" Mexican beaded lizard, and the clouded anole—another lizard, and the favorite prey of the blunt-headed tree snake.

Like other forests of the world, vast areas of tropical deciduous forest in the Americas have been cut into, cleared, and converted to grazing lands or other agricultural uses over many decades. The tropical deciduous forest in southern Sonora and northern Sinaloa is recognized as one of the best preserved of its type, and nongovernmental organizations in Mexico and the United States, including the Arizona-Sonora Desert Museum, are working to conserve what is left.

Ken Stockton
"Along the Río Mayo"
oil, 23" x 35"

Near the old colonial town of Alamos in southern Sonora, one of the largest remaining tracts of tropical deciduous forest in the New World still thrives.

Species/Subspecies of the Sonoran Desert Region
Now Considered Extinct

Mammals
Ángel de la Guarda deer mouse *(Peromyscus guarda guarda)*
Anthony's woodrat *(Neotoma anthonyi)*
Bailey's pocket mouse *(Chaetodipus baileyi fornicatus)*
Bunker's woodrat *(Neotoma bunkeri)*
Estanque Island deer mouse *(Peromyscus guarda* subsp. indet.*)*
Harbison's deer mouse *(Peromyscus guarda harbisoni)*
Intermountain wolf *(Canis lupus youngi)*
Mejia Island deer mouse *(Peromyscus guarda mejiae)*
Merriam's elk *(Cervus elaphus merriami)*
Mexican grizzly bear *(Ursus arctos nelsoni)*
Pemberton's deer mouse *(Peromyscus pembertoni)*
Sonoran river otter *(Lontra canadensis sonorae)*
San Jose Island Kangaroo Rat *(Dipodomys insularis)*
San Martín Island woodrat *(Neotoma martinensis)*
San Roque Island deer mouse *(Peromyscus maniculatus cineritius)*
Slevin's deer mouse *(Peromyscus slevini)*
Turner woodrat *(Neotoma albigula varia)*

Birds
Imperial woodpecker *(Campephilus imperialis)*

Fish
Monkey Springs pupfish/Santa Cruz pupfish *(Cyprinodon arcuatus)*

Plants
Ballona cinquefoil *(Potentilla multijuga)*
Frosted mint *(Poliomintha incana)*
Parish's bush mallow *(Malacothamnus parishii)*
Parish's gooseberry *(Ribes divaricatum var. parishii)*
Parish's sunflower *(Helianthus nuttallii parishii)*
Pringle's monardella *(Monardella pringlei)*
Sonoran neststraw, mesquite neststraw *(Stylocline sonorensis)*
Twin desert-dandelion *(Malacothrix similes)*

Nearly two dozen additional species/subspecies have been extirpated from Arizona or the Sonoran Desert north of the U.S.-Mexico border.

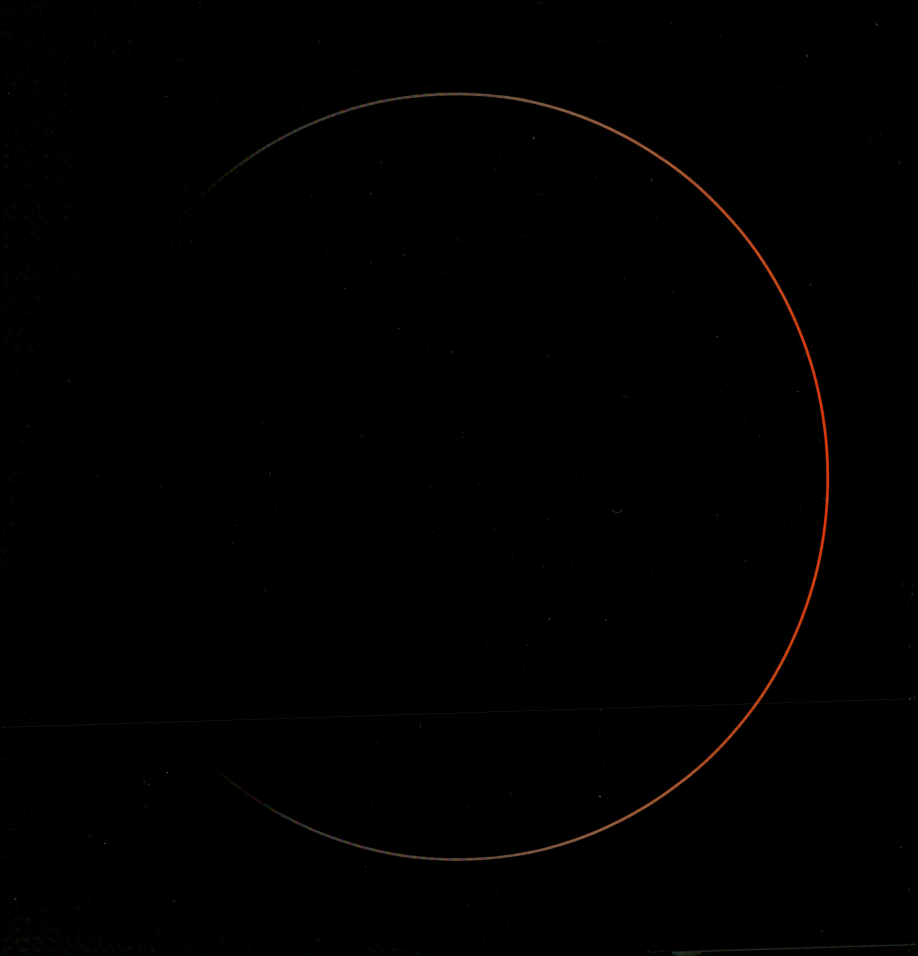

Conservation Work at the Arizona-Sonora Desert Museum

Richard C. Brusca, Ph.D.
Senior Director, Science and Conservation, Arizona-Sonora Desert Museum

The Arizona-Sonora Desert Museum, a nonprofit research and education institution based in Tucson, Arizona, is a combination zoological park, botanical garden, nature education center, and conservation organization. Our multiple functions are reflected in our memberships in the Association of Zoos and Aquariums, American Association of Museums, American Public Gardens Association (formerly American Association of Botanical Gardens and Arboreta), Center for Plant Conservation, and others. Our primary mission is to understand and interpret the natural history of the Sonoran Desert Region, and to promote science-based conservation in the region, which encompasses the Sonoran Desert and adjacent biomes, including numerous contained or nearby mountain ranges, Mexico's northern thornscrub and tropical deciduous forest, and the Gulf of California and its islands.

At the Desert Museum, live animals and plants native to the Sonoran Desert Region are integrated into outdoor settings designed to replicate their natural habitat. The Museum is unique in the "zoo world" for its strong interpretive and conservation focus on *ecological processes* rather than on individual species. For example, the Museum's Pollination Gardens interpret the interaction of animals and plants and the reciprocal benefits of pollination ecology, rather than simply talking about, say, hummingbirds or ocotillos. Conservation of the ecosystems in this region is the ultimate goal for all our research and educational programs.

The Desert Museum's conservation efforts mainly promote *in-situ* conservation (i.e., the conservation of nature in place, as opposed to a traditional botanical garden or zoo) focusing on the protection of natural communities more than on preservation of individual species. For example, Museum research on the ecology of desert ironwood trees attracted the attention of the U.S. Department of the Interior and was instrumental in the creation of Arizona's Ironwood Forest National Monument in 2000. Museum staff conduct biological inventories and assessments of this national monument and other national parks and monuments in the Southwest to help the Bureau of Land Management and National Park Service develop their natural resources management plans. More recently, the Museum has worked with other nonprofit organizations to help establish a new nature reserve in southern Sonora (Mexico), near the colonial town of Alamos, where one of the last remaining large stands of tropical deciduous forest still flourishes. Closer to "home," the Museum also participated in the science planning for the award-winning Pima County Sonoran Desert Conservation Plan in southern Arizona.

On its grounds, the Desert Museum sustains populations of several federally listed threatened and endangered vertebrate species, such as the Mexican gray wolf, thick-billed parrot, ocelot, and more than twenty species of native fishes. The Museum also runs a captive breeding program for the endangered San Esteban chuckwalla. Its Botany Department maintains cultures of several endangered plant species, including Nichol's Turk's head cactus, Pima pineapple cactus, and the flowering shrub Kearney's bluestar. Since 1979, the Museum has cultivated the Nichol's Turk's head cactus, studying its fruit and seed to determine fecundity and other qualities effecting viability.

The Museum's Research and Conservation Department staff participate in numerous field projects that involve endangered and threatened species and habitats. The Migratory Pollinators Program strives to understand the threats to migratory birds and bats that are important pollinators across our landscape—among them, the endangered lesser long-nosed bat (a key pollinator for columnar cactuses, such as saguaro), rufous hummingbird, and white-winged dove. Evidence indicates that populations of these and other pollinator species are declining due to habitat destruction throughout their range. The Migratory Pollinators Program is mapping migration corridors between southern Mexico and the United States, and is identifying the major floral food resources that fuel these migrations. Our recommendations of critical habitat for protection and preservation of these, and other threatened species, have led to significant conservation initiatives in Mexico and the Southwest.

> THE MUSEUM IS UNIQUE IN THE "ZOO WORLD" FOR ITS STRONG INTERPRETIVE AND CONSERVATION FOCUS ON ECOLOGICAL PROCESSES.

The Museum's research in the Gulf of California (Sea of Cortez) and its coastal habitats has played key roles in developing conservation strategies for critical coastal and island habitats, as well as the Colorado River delta region, including protection of coastal wetlands. Our online All-Animal Database for the Gulf of California (7,000+ species) is an unparalleled resource, the first of its kind for any region on Earth; it is being used to identify conservation hotspots in and around the Gulf, and to develop management plans for protected areas.

The Museum's award-winning publication arm, the ASDM Press, produces science-based popular and technical books, field guides, bilingual children's books, and other publications that inform a broad audience on matters of conservation importance for the region (www.desertmuseum.org/books).

For 60 years the Arizona-Sonora Desert Museum has been a leader in understanding and protecting critical habitats in the Sonoran Desert Region. The creation of the Museum's Art Institute in 1998 (originally called the School of Natural History Art, taking its current name in 2003) and the Vanishing Circles art-for-conservation initiative are reflections of the Museum's profound dedication and far-reaching, innovative efforts to inspire people to live in harmony with the natural world.

The Vanishing Circles Collection

Michael Baldwin
Trustee, Arizona-Sonora Desert Museum

*V*anishing Circles is a collection of paintings and drawings acquired for the Arizona-Sonora Desert Museum by the Priscilla and Michael Baldwin Foundation. Over the last several years, works by artists well known for their skills have been commissioned by the foundation. Each of the animals, plants, and habitats portrayed in this collection is endangered, threatened, or otherwise compromised in the Sonora Desert Region. In a few cases, a portrayed species may not be in danger in another region but will have all but disappeared in the Sonoran Desert Region due to habitat destruction or one of the many other environmental impacts that civilization has brought upon the natural world.

In commissioning the works for the Vanishing Circles Collection, the Baldwin Foundation sought artistic media and stylistic approaches that draw the viewer back to the original purpose of natural-history art. In the eighteenth century, the eminent botanist and botanical artist Joseph Banks accompanied Captain James Cook on the HM *Endeavor* Expedition to the Pacific. Banks' paintings and drawings are still on view in the Natural History Museum in London and are occasionally in traveling exhibits. His original purpose was to portray specimens as they appeared fresh to the eye, in a scientifically accurate manner. The original plant specimens from this expedition are also exhibited, but they bear little resemblance to the living plants painted by Banks. It is only through his vibrant renderings that we have any notion of how he found them.

In the making of a scientific illustration or an artistic portrayal (the two are distinct, informative art forms) a creature or a plant may be shown in a choice of poses, by itself or in its natural habitat. A vast choice of activities and backgrounds is available to the artist, and the unique character of the subject may be vibrantly depicted by a focus on detail or an appropriate backdrop. In many cases it is not possible to photograph particular species *in situ*, in the wild in natural attitudes, due to their scarcity, elusive nature, nocturnal habits, etc. But the artist is not bound to work *in situ* and is able to portray the subject to its best advantage using a variety of reference sources, including multiple photographs or museum specimens.

The 27 artists in this collection were chosen for their affinity with a particular natural area, or by their floral or faunal leanings: the fauna has been painted by artists known and respected for their work depicting animals,

EXTINCTION IS A FINAL STATE OF BEING FROM WHICH THERE CAN BE NO RECOVERY, NO GOING BACK, AND NO GOING FORWARD.

the flora by prominent botanical artists, and the habitats by well-known artists accomplished in landscape painting. To date, the collection includes works by John Agnew, Edward Aldrich, Priscilla Baldwin, Carel Brest van Kempen, Bobbie Brooks, Adele Earnshaw, Larry Fanning, Scott Fraser, Joe Garcia, Janet Heaton, William Hook, Rachel Ivanyi, Shari Jones, Les Lull, Joan McGann, Dulce Nascimento, Rhonda Nass, Anne Peyton, Martiena Richter, Michael Riddet, Constance Sayas, Manabu Saito, John Seerey-Lester, Richard Sloan, Ken Stockton, Livia Vieira, and Nicholas Wilson. All share a common interest in preserving the natural environment.

The Vanishing Circles Collection is meant to focus the viewer's attention on the beauty and value of the region by concentrating the gaze on the details and relationships of its many parts—on the inhabitants and their habitat. Each subject, from the little frog to the large and spectacular vista, has a unique appeal and an important role to play. If the migration path of the tiniest pollinator is blocked by an alteration of the landscape, an entire plant species and those creatures dependent on it could be put in jeopardy. Species, ecosystems, and habitats are interconnected in the circle of life; hence the term "Vanishing Circles."

To understand the vulnerability of ecosystems, consider that each of the wondrous creatures and habitats in this exhibit are in danger of disappearing or have already vanished from the Sonoran Desert Region, interrupting a circle of life. We hope that this exhibit will inspire in its viewers a sense of urgency to act for conservation and preservation. The present Vanishing Circles Collection is but a beginning; there will be additions to the collection at the Arizona-Sonora Desert Museum. Through its classes, programs, and exhibitions, the Museum's Art Institute strives to increase awareness of the fragility of the Sonoran Desert Region. We hope that increased attention to these threatened lands will slow the loss of habitats and species and focus attention on the value of the region's remarkably rich biodiversity. We hope that people from other regions who see this show or peruse this catalogue will also be inspired to embrace the concept of "conservation through art education."

Extinction is a final state of being from which there can be no recovery, no going back, and no going forward.

The Artists

The artists of the Vanishing Circles exhibit are listed alphabetically, with the subjects or titles of their paintings in italics above their names.

desert tortoise, Gila monster, Ramsey Canyon leopard frog, "Waiting for Rain" – Altar Valley
John N. Agnew
www.johnnagnew.com
http://herps2art.wordpress.com

After receiving a Bachelor of Fine Arts degree from the University of Cincinnati, John Agnew concentrated on a career in exhibit design for natural history museums, and in the early 1980s finally took up fine  art full time. He still produces murals for museums and zoos, but he is better known for his smaller works of reptiles, amphibians, birds, and landscapes. His work is in collections worldwide, and has hung in the U.S. embassies in Belarus and Costa Rica; in the United States he has exhibited in national juried shows such as those of the Society of Animal Artists, Artists for Conservation, and the Leigh Yawkey Woodson Art Museum in Wisconsin, including its *Birds in Art* exhibit. Agnew has won multiple awards in national and regional shows.

Statement: I have always had an interest in reptiles and amphibians, going back to a childhood interest in dinosaurs. Being able to work with them is a great privilege. My work in natural history museums and in scientific illustration has nurtured a very realistic style in my art, and I love doing the detail of a reptile's scales or a bird's feathers, but I also find that under every good realist painting is a good abstract.

bald eagle, California brown pelican, ocelot, osprey, thick-billed parrot
Edward Aldrich
e.aldrich@comcast.net
www.edwardaldrich.com

Painting primarily in oils, Edward Aldrich depicts wildlife from around the world. He graduated from the Rhode Island School of Design and at the age of 26 was juried into the Society of Animal Artists. His work is frequently included in their annual *Art and the Animal* exhibitions. His art is carried in galleries across the western United States and is held in many permanent collections, including the Leigh Yawkey Woodson Art Museum, where he regularly participates in the prestigious *Birds in Art* show. His paintings are consistently included in national shows such as the Gilcrease Museum's *American Art in Miniature,* the National Wildlife Art Museum's *Western Visions Miniature and More,* the Rockwell Museum's *Representing Representation,* and the *Oil Painters of America National Show*. His artwork has been featured in such national publications as *Southwest Art, Wildlife Art,* and *American Artist*. In his book *Drawing and Painting Animals*, Aldrich outlines his artistic processes for artists of varying levels of experience.

Statement: For me, this exhibit was a great opportunity to depict species I rarely get to work with—species that offer wonderful image potential due to their interesting and diverse appearances. I am proud to work  with organizations and programs that support wildlife conservation like the Arizona-Sonora Desert Museum and the Lynx Reintroduction Program in Colorado.

black-tailed prairie dog
Priscilla Baldwin
pavb@baldwinp.com

Having lived in South Africa, Texas, Hawaii, Colorado, and Arizona, Priscilla Baldwin has known and explored diverse landscapes and wild environments. She earned a B.A. degree from Sweetbriar College, Virginia, and has long pursued her passion for gardening, architectural design, and art of the natural world—particularly botanical art. Baldwin is founder of the Arizona-Sonora Desert Museum's Art Institute in Tucson, Arizona, and has served on the Museum's Board of Trustees. She has also served on the board of the American Society of Botanical Artists. Her art has been featured in numerous publications; it  hangs in many private and corporate collections and is held in the permanent collections of the Arizona-Sonora Desert Museum and the Hunt Institute for Botanical Documentation.

Statement: My favorite subjects are the ordinary and mundane parts of the natural world, which are often overlooked for some reason. I like to show the beauty and uniqueness of each subject and bring attention to it, so the viewer may see it in a new light and with fresh eyes.

California condor, desert tortoise, giant spotted whiptail, Mexican beaded lizard, San Esteban chuckwalla, spotted bat
Carel P. Brest van Kempen
PO Box 17647; Holladay, UT 84117
cpbvk@juno.com
http://rigorvitae.blogspot.com
www.cpbrestvankempen.com
www.rigorvitae.net

Carel Pieter Brest van Kempen has spent brief periods living in many places, but has never felt compelled to move his stereo out of Salt Lake County, Utah, where he was born and raised. A self-taught artist, he has painted full-time since 1989. He is a member of the Society of Animal Artists, which selected him in 2008 as a "Master Member," an honored bestowed to only 14 artists. The Society has also awarded him with six Awards of Excellence. In conjunction with the 2002 Olympics, he was named a "Most Honored Artist of Utah" by the Springville Museum of Art. His work has been exhibited worldwide in such venues as the Smithsonian Institution, the American Museum of Natural History, the British Museum, and the National Taiwan Museum. He has illustrated a number of books and has recently authored one.

Statement: As ecology is the engine that drives evolution, so is it the motivating force behind my work. As a visual artist, I'm concerned with form, but as a naturalist it is function that fascinates me, and my work explores the relationship between the two. When I select a subject, I typically try to find a way to display as articulately as I can the qualities that make that species unique, and how those qualities function in an ecological setting. Every technical aspect of the painting—composition, palette, scale, etc., hopefully serves to emphasize this point.

For the beaded lizard painting, I decided to depict a typical behavior: climbing to a bird's nest, in this case, a mourning dove's. I used a curved perspective in order to give a sense of ascension while still showing the lizard's habitat. In the desert tortoise paintig, a male prepares to charge a rival, who exists as little more than a suggestion in the painting. Never having seen the San Esteban chuckwalla outside of the Desert Museum, I relied largely on my knowledge of the common chuckwalla to paint that piece. It is the distinctive style of whiptail locomotion that I tried to capture in the giant spotted whiptail painting, with the reptile sliding, snakelike, down the surface of a smooth rock. I also decided to take a break from hot, arid settings and place this subject in a shady riverbed. I cropped the California condor in that painting, just slightly, to suggest the great mass that characterizes this species. Spotted bats tend to forage at a decent height, so I placed the apex of a mountain promontory in the piece to give it more compositional interest, with just a suggestion of the tops of ponderosa pines.

Sabo's pincushion cactus, Bristol's hedgehog cactus
Bobbie Brown
40W950 S. Bridle Creek Dr.
St. Charles, Illinois 60175
630-377-5239
bobbiebrownartist@hotmail.com

A signature member of the Pennsylvania Watercolor Society, the Philadelphia Water Color Society, and the Colored Pencil Society of America, Bobbie studied landscape painting at the Pennsylvania Academy of Fine Arts and is a graduate of the Botanical Art Certificate Program of The Morton Arboretum. Her work has been published in *Today's Botanical Artists* and has been exhibited widely in juried and invitational shows, including those of the American Society of Botanical Artists, American Watercolor Society, National Watercolor Society, and the Colored Pencil Society of America. Her paintings are included in public and private collections throughout the United States and in Great Britain and Japan.

She was commissioned by Ball Horticultural Company to do a series of botanical paintings for their Centennial Collection and by the breeder of the 'Purple Wave' petunia in Japan to portray its introduction. Brown teaches botanical art at The Morton Arboretum in Lisle, Illinois.

Statement: In researching Sabo's pincushion cactus, I had the privilege of witnessing and recording in photographs the progression from one bloom through nine at a time, with multiple stages of buds. I chose to include all of those "small miracles" unfolding in my painting, striving to be scientifically accurate while artistically conveying its delicate beauty. With the hedgehog, I studied the buds, flowers, and spines with a magnifying glass. I was fascinated by how much the plants changed from day to day, as buds swelled and opened. I hope that my artistic interpretation will emphasize the value and necessity of protecting these treasures.

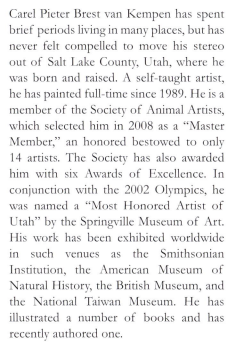

violet-crowned hummingbird
Adele Earnshaw
adele.earnshaw@gmail.com,
www.AdeleEarnshaw.com

A sixth generation New Zealander, Adele Earnshaw immigrated with her family to the United States as a young woman, but her childhood in New Zealand has been a major influence on her work and subject matter. Earnshaw's work has been exhibited at the American Museum of Natural History in New York and has toured Japan and Sweden. In addition to designing the first three stamps for the New Zealand Game Bird Habitat Stamp Program, she was selected as a judge for the 2003 Federal Duck Stamp Competition held at the U. S. Department of Interior's Fish and Wildlife Service in Washington D.C. In 2000 she was one of twelve artists invited  to participate in the Eco-art Conference and Exhibition in Taiwan, where her work was exhibited at the National Taiwan Museum in Taipei. Earnshaw has been a full-time artist for more than twenty years, and works from her home in Oak Creek Canyon, Arizona.

Statement: After many years of living in northern Arizona, hummingbirds continue to fascinate me. In this painting, rather than paint a bird portrait, I show the tiny violet-crowned hummingbird in a very large world.

"Mexican gray wolves," northern aplomado falcon
Larry Fanning
Larry Fanning Studios LLC
800-859-1742
303-674-0749

A self-taught artist, Larry Fanning has been interested in art throughout his life, but has also pursued a variety of vocations and avocations, including work as a radio talk-show host, an ordained minister,  and a motivational lecturer. He began his art career as a commercial artist for the Boeing Company, and at the age of 50 he began to focus strictly on a fine-art career, painting for exclusive galleries and private collectors. Fanning paints in a vivid representational style, covering a myriad of Western and wildlife subjects including scenes of cowboys living on the American frontier and Native American culture, which have garnered numerous awards. Fanning is also recognized for his renderings of gray wolves, elk, moose, deer, and exotic wild animals, as well as portraits. His work has been displayed at prestigious art shows throughout the United States.

Statement: I am very interested in the conservation of endangered species in the American Southwest, and I chose these two subjects to lend my support for their preservation.

shell spiral
Scott Fraser
303-772-0521
www.sfraser.com
scottfraser126@gmail.com

Scott Fraser pursued his formal art education at the Kansas City Art Institute and the University of Colorado at Denver. His work is represented in the collections of many museums—among them, the Metropolitan Museum of Art, the Denver Art Museum, Colorado Springs Fine Arts Center, Amarillo Museum of Art, Arnot Art Museum, Museum of New Mexico, and the Philbrook Museum of Art in Tulsa. He has had a dozen solo exhibitions in galleries from New York to Colorado, and has been included in group exhibitions at many of the same venues, as well as the Van Vechten-Lineberry Taos Art Museum, Riverside Art Museum (California), Knoxville Museum, and Butler Institute of American Art in Youngstown (Ohio), among  others. His work has been in dozens of publications, including: *The Artist's Magazine, American Arts Quarterly, American Artist, American Art Collector,* and *ARTnews*, and has been featured on the cover of *Southwest Art*.

Statement: I have used the spiral as a concept in several paintings over the years. I like it as a design element to draw the viewer's eye towards the center of the piece. By presenting them in this configuration I am echoing the patterns of many of the shells themselves. The nautilus shell is in the shape of a logarithmic spiral, as defined by Fibonacci and the "golden equation." This formulation is found in many elements of nature, including leaf arrangements on plants and the patterning on a pineapple.

Abert's towhee, masked bobwhite
Joe Garcia
www.joegarcia.com,
info@joegarcia.com
760-765-2067

Native Californian, Joe Garcia earned a Bachelor of Fine Arts degree with an emphasis on advertising and illustration from the Art Center College of Design in Los Angeles. He worked as an illustrator and graphic designer for 13 years, but he eventually left the commercial work behind and began painting full-time. Garcia's art has appeared in numerous magazines, including *Southwest Art, The Artist's Magazine, Wildlife Art,* and *Watercolor Magic.* North Light Books produced his books *Mastering the Watercolor Wash* and the *Watercolor Bible.* His original paintings and prints may be seen in galleries and private collections throughout the United States and in Canada, New Zealand, and Europe.

Statement: Raised on a small ranch in Southern California, I have always felt a great affinity with Mother Nature. My career evolved from commercial art to a fine art focusing on landscapes and wildlife, and I became part of the community of artists who paint such rewarding subjects. As scenes change and species vanish, we become the visual historians of the future. I am honored to have my paintings included in the Vanishing Circles collection.

"*High Flying Brown Pelicans: Where the Desert Meets the Sea*" – California brown pelican
Janet Heaton
Heatonstudio@aol.com
561-622-8848

Great museums in Europe and childhood experiences in pristine lands of old Florida gave Janet Heaton an appreciation for art and nature. But not until the age of 40, when she joined a painting class, did she embark on a career in art. She

expanded her studies and media explorations, and soon found a passion for portraying wildlife. Early on, the wild creatures of Florida and, later, African wildlife became her favored subjects. Heaton's works are held in dozens of private and public collections, and have hung in many museums and galleries, including The Witte Museum in San Antonio, the Cleveland Museum of Natural History, the National Arts Club in New York, and the National Geographic Society in Washington D.C. Heaton's works have been repeatedly juried into the Leigh Yawkey Woodson Art Museum's *Bird in Art* shows, and she has work in its permanent collection. Her art has appeared in numerous publications, including *The New York Art Review, African Wildlife and Art, Pastel Journal, American Arts,* and *This Earth: American Women and Nature.*

Statement: Knowing and liking my subjects helps me create better images, since all of the sights and sounds of the animals and their natural environment are what make a painting whole. When I was invited to paint the brown pelican, I questioned whether pelicans lived in the desert; I soon learned that the Sonoran Desert includes and embraces the Sea of Cortez. Fortunately, I see brown pelicans, since I live on the coast of Florida where they are seen in abundance.

"*Ironwood Tree*" – desert ironwood tree, "*Line in the Sand*" – Algodones Dunes, "*Mangrove Bay*" and "*Tropic of Cancer*" – Sea of Cortez, "*Organ Pipe*" – organ pipe cactus
William Hook

www.williamhook.net   hookstudio@comcast.net

Through the influence of his father and grandmother, a professional photographer and architect respectively, art became second nature to William Hook. He received his Bachelor of Fine Arts from the University of New Mexico and studied at the Universita Italiana Per Straniere in Perugia, Italy, with MFA study at the Art Center College of Design, Los Angeles. He has received numerous awards for his work, including Best Local Artist at the Carmel Plein Aire Festival (2003), National Academy of Design's Acrylic Artist of the Year Award (1996), and the National Parks' Arts for the Parks Best Landscape Award (1993). Hook's paintings are included in many museums; among them, the Denver Art Museum, The Forbes Gallery (New York), and the University of New Mexico Art Museum. His work is included in corporate and private collections worldwide, including those of AOL/Time Warner; Erivan & Helga Haub Western Art Collection (Germany); Forbes Magazine; and Texaco World Headquarters.

Statement: Painting the ironwood tree and the organ pipe cactus gave me the rare circumstance to paint parts of the desert I probably would not normally paint. The pristine beauty of Organ Pipe Cactus National Monument is unparalleled. In my painting of that remote location, the viewer looks toward the distant mountains in Mexico. The "Tropic of Cancer" ocean scene and the sand dunes embrace the breadth of the Sonoran Desert; both were painted in my studio from photographs I made. The Tropic of Cancer runs right through the tip of the Baja peninsula. "Mangrove Bay" portrays a spot in San Lucas Bay, Guaymas, Mexico. The dunes painting depicts a scene from atop a dune looking down on the only highway that traverses this area. It is, remarkably, the line of demarcation between barren sand and the beginning of the Imperial Valley on the California side.

American crocodile, Arizona trout, cactus ferruginous pygmy owl, fishes of the Colorado River, fishes of the Gila River, fishes of the Rio Yaqui, pupfish, sea turtles, true frogs

Rachel Ivanyi
Rachel Ivanyi Illustration
2433 W. Placita de Ramo
Tucson, AZ 85741   520-437-8169
rivanyi@comcast.net, www.rachelivanyi.com

Rachel Ivanyi is a freelance, natural-science illustrator who works on a variety of natural history subjects, but specializes in reptiles and amphibians. She received a Bachelor of Science degree in zoology from the University of California at Davis and Graduate Certification in Natural Science Illustration from the University of California at Santa Cruz. Although Ivanyi originally aimed for a career as a wildlife vet, she soon realized that she preferred drawing birds to treating them medically. Her work can be found in a variety of textbooks, science magazines, children's books, and field guides. Many of her illustrations and paintings are also produced as archival pigment prints. Her clients include *National Geographic*, *Scientific American*, McGraw-Hill, and the Arizona-Sonora Desert Museum.

Statement: Long ago, I was drawn to scientific illustration by beautiful historical natural-history illustrations of amphibians. My favorite is the hand-colored copper engraving on the cover of Roesel von Rosenhof's *Historia Naturalis Ranarum*, 1758, which is a splendid composition of Old World plants and animals—most of which are amphibians. When working on the group of true frogs, having an appreciation and an eye for the minutia allowed me to showcase the subtle differences between these species. In reality, I enjoy the research into their natural history almost as much as illustrating them.

A series of owls in pen and ink was the first project on my new career path 18 years ago, but my passion for owls lives on. I particularly enjoyed creating the scene in the desert ironwood with the pygmy owl eyeing its next meal. Before painting the sea turtles, I was fortunate to get behind the scenes of the Aquarium of the Pacific in Long Beach, California, to observe green sea turtles just inches from my nose. Watching them move so gracefully, as if flying through liquid air, inspired me to portray that movement in my painting. I also included some of their favorite foods. For the American crocodile, I created a model scene out of clay to get an idea of perspective and composition, as I often do before painting. Illustrating the detail in the wide variety of the crocodile's scale types was especially fascinating.

Illustrating the delicate yet pugnacious pupfishes involved studying species descriptions and specimens from the University of Arizona's (unfortunately lifeless) ichthyology collection. I hope that the color and life in these paintings serves to remind people of these precious gems in our desert waterways. With their remarkable adaptations to fast-water living (like embedded scales and prominent humps), the Colorado River fishes were some of the most interesting species I worked with. The pikeminnow and razorback suckers at the Desert Museum afforded me ample opportunities to watch these rare fish swim. Scales were a common element in several of my paintings, and I relished getting lost in the magnificent scale details of the Gila and Yaqui River fishes. I presented them in a traditional style reminiscent of biological illustrations of the past; but with these paintings I wasn't obliged to show a complete side view of the fish, and could play with their fins and body positions to create a tad more lively gesture. Because the trout have bodies that curve appreciably as they swim, I could depict them this way without being unnatural, showing one species flowing into the other—a welcome variation.

San Pedro River
Shari Jones
720-771-8631
sjonesdnvr@earthlink.net

For much of her professional career, Shari Jones worked in graphic design and illustration, but in recent years she returned to a focus on painting and drawing, concentrating on subjects in Arizona and Colorado. Before retiring from the graphics industry, she designed publications and packaging, billboards, and convention display. Jones designed for commercial enterprises in Colorado, as well as for individual clients. She created designs for businesses and organizations like the Colorado Dude and Guest Ranch Association, Denver Wholesale Florists, Coors Brewing Company, Applewood Seed Company, and the Energy Corporation of America. Her fine art has been shown in various exhibition venues, including those of the Arizona Plein Air Painters, Mesa Art League, Denver Botanic Gardens, Art Students League of Denver, and Arizona-Sonora Desert Museum.

Statement: Nature offers a bounty of beauty wherever one looks. That beauty is my inspiration for painting and drawing. My goal as an artist is to represent nature's wonders and bring that beauty to others. One of the blessings of being an artist is seeing the details as well as the grand expanses.

As the world moves ever faster, we must take the time to see and value the beauty around us.

"Riparian Respite" – San Pedro River
Les Lull
leslull@gmail.com
www.lullstudios.com
480-628-1122

Les Lull grew up in rural South Dakota farm country, where he was strongly influenced by his grandfather, a German craftsman. The predominant element of wood in his childhood prompted an appreciation for trees, a common theme in his work. Lull studied fine art at Black Hills State University. His work has been selected for the Top 100 in PaintAmerica Association's national *Paint the Parks* competition. He also had five works selected for the Top 100 and Mini 50 for subsequent Paint America exhibitions in Topeka, Kansas. His paintings have been on display at the Kolb Studio in the Grand Canyon.

Statement: My work is about childhood curiosities and exploration—finding a good tree to climb, a mud puddle to splash in, a pile of cast-aside antiquities, or a wooded glen to explore. I hope my paintings spark the imagination of the viewer and initiate a flood of memories. I am particularly fond of Henry David Thoreau's words conveying the magnetism of trees: "I frequently tramped eight or ten miles through the deepest snow to keep an appointment with a beech tree, or a yellow birch, or an old acquaintance among the pines."

Pima pineapple cactus
Joan McGann
jmcgann@mcgannland.com

Joan McGann received a Bachelor of Fine Arts in lithography and drawing from Wichita State University, as well as a Certificate of Excellence in the Nature Illustration Program of the Arizona-Sonora Desert Museum's Art Institute. Her botanical art has been featured in Tucson at the Tucson Botanical Gardens, the Desert Museum, and Tohono Chul Park. Her work has also been part of national exhibits, including the International Juried Exhibition of the American Society of Botanical Artists and The Horticultural Society of New York (2008, 2009, 2010); the Ninth Annual Botanical Art Exhibition at The Filoli Center, Woodside, California; and the 2005 Guild of Natural Science Illustrators Juried Exhibition in Eugene, Oregon. McGann's works are in the permanent collection of the Hunt Institute for Botanical Documentation at Carnegie Mellon University in Pennsylvania.

Statement: Since moving to Tucson in 1980, I have loved the desert environment, even more so since I started drawing and learning about its amazing plants. Their volumes and forms are very conducive to my drawing style. At the Desert Museum I was able to draw and photograph the Pima pineapple cactus to advantage with the help of its botanists, who kept me posted on when the cactus was budding and blooming so I wouldn't miss its short bloom cycle.

Kearny sumac
Dulce Nascimento
www.dulcenascimento.com.br
55-21-25353614/ 55-21-25792795/
55-21-98013909

Born in Rio de Janeiro, Ducle Nascimento earned a Bachelor of Arts in landscape design. She studied botanical illustration with Maria Werneck de Castro and perfected her technique at the Royal Botanic Gardens, Kew, with Christabel King, as a scholar of the Margaret Mee Botanical Foundation. She participated in a number of botanical expeditions through various Brazilian ecosystems to draw and paint the plant species in their habitat. Some of these renderings have been used on postage stamps. Every year for the past 12 years she has given art classes on a boat in the Amazon and she has lived in Pará in the Amazon for nearly two years. Her paintings were chosen to be the presents of the State from presidents of Brazil to Queen Elizabeth II, the King and Queen of Spain, and the King and Queen of Norway.

Statement: Illustrating plants helps create a sympathy and appreciation for nature, and it is rewarding to know that registering the flora of a land will help preserve the environment. It is both a responsibility and a pleasure to illustrate new species or vulnerable species, such as *Rhus kearneyi*. I hope that these paintings will bring more attention to rare plants and lead scientists to investigate and discover anything from cures for diseases to their unique role in the ecosystem.

desert night-blooming cereus, Pima pineapple cactus
Rhonda Nass
608-370-654
rnass@charter.net
www.rnass.com

As a teenager Rhonda Nass was already bent on becoming an artist, in large part because a high school art teacher said she couldn't be one. She received a degree in art education at the University of Wisconsin, Madison. For more than thirty years, she and her husband, Rick, have operated an art/illustration business, now based in Prairie du Sac, Wisconsin. Nass works in a highly realistic style, focusing predominately on nature and natural history subjects. Her work is exhibited and collected internationally, including venues such as the Carnegie Mellon University's Hunt Institute for Botanical Documentation. Her work appears in numerous publications including *Atlantic Monthly*, *Communication Arts*, and the textbook, *Biology of Plants*.

Statement: I came to the southern Arizona desert for the first time to see live examples of the Pima pineapple cactus and night-blooming cereus. Coming from the Midwest, I was struck by a "live-in-the-moment" sense of the desert plants' preciousness and urgency—plants that bloomed seldom and briefly. I watched in awe in the middle of the night as the night-blooming cereus strutted its stuff during its two-hour opening scene. (I would be thrilled if this painting communicated even a smidgen of the beauty of this "queen of the night.") The Pima pineapple cactus specimens that I came to observe and photograph bloomed with great panache only hours before my departure. Both plants showcase what I discovered to be a majesty of the desert.

"Eye to the Sky" – burrowing owls
Anne Peyton
www.annepeytonart.com

For 20 years, Anne Peyton's art focused on motorsports, depicting all types of racing vehicles. Now, she has turned her eye and hand to the natural world, still emphasizing the representation of action. Based in the Ahwatukee Foothills of Arizona, she is a member of the National Oil and Acrylic Painters' Society (honored with Signature Artist's Guild status in 2004) and the American Society of Marine Artists. She is an associate member of the National Society of Painters in Casein and Acrylic, and a signature member of the Society of Animal Artists and Artists for Conservation. Peyton's work has been seen in exhibitions such as: *Birds in Art* at the Leigh Yawkey Woodson Art Museum in Wisconsin; *Arts for the Parks* in Jackson, Wyoming; *Western Visions Miniatures and More* at the National Museum of Wildlife Art in Jackson Hole; National Society of Painters in Casein & Acrylic annual exhibition at the Salmagundi Club, New York City; and numerous Society of Animal Artists exhibitions.

Statement: There are two criteria for my paintings. One is that the final image shows respect for the subject; the second is that viewers can learn something by studying the art. Before creating my burrowing owl painting, I went into the field to capture photos of owls, appropriate mountain ranges for the background, and thunderstorms for the sky. As ground-dwelling birds, burrowing owls need to be concerned with ground predators, but also need to be vigilant about sky predators like hawks. That is why I chose "Eye to the Sky" for a title. It is actions and their meanings that I want to convey to the viewer.

"Forest Dweller" – margay
Martiena Richter
mrichterscbd@hotmail.com
www.martienarichter.com
630-335-4174.

A self-taught artist with a fulltime career in wildlife art, Martiena Richter first discovered the magic of scratchboard engraving in 1974, and scratchboard, with its exacting intricate detail and sharp contrast, has been her medium of choice ever since. Richter is a member of the Society of Animal Artists headquartered in New York City. Her engravings have received numerous awards and honors. Most recently she was juried into the 2009 Society of Animal Artists *Art and the Animal Annual Exhibition*, and was selected for its National Museum Tour. She received the Leggett & Platt and Founder's Awards at the 2008 Mid-

west Gathering of the Artists in Carthage, Missouri, and she was selected as "Artist of the Year" for the 2009 Southern Wildlife Festival in Decatur, Alabama. She participates in several juried art shows each year and her limited edition prints are sold throughout the United States.

Statement: Scratch-board engraving is the perfect medium to depict the margay. The black background works perfectly for the cat's black spots and its nocturnal setting. After using a sharp knife to engrave texture and intricate detail, I use brush and watercolor to add a dimension of color. Here, I was able to show the wonderful texture and intricate detail of its fur and the luminosity of its golden brown eyes using this engraving technique. Cats are one of my favorite subjects, and I wanted to pay tribute to this little-known small cat.

Huachuca giant skipper, least Bell's vireo, Merriam's mouse, rufous-winged sparrow, Sonoran tiger salamander, Tarahumara frog, yellow-billed cuckoo
Michael James Riddet
www.riddetstudio.com

Although already painting in a representational style, Riddet pursued a degree in biology from Roosevelt University in Chicago. He later secured a job as an artist-naturalist, combining his skills in art and interest in natural history, and finally embarked on a career as a full-time artist in 1979. Today, his clients include National and International Wildlife magazines, Sports Afield, the Franklin Mint, and Random House. Riddet's work has been shown in museums and institutions in the United States and abroad. For 14 years, his work has been selected into the annual Leigh Yawkey Woodson Art Museum's prestigious Birds in Art exhibition, and three of his works are in its permanent collection. In 1996, he was elected into the Society of Animal Artists, from which he received an Award of Excellence. In 2001, he was elected into Chicago's Palette & Chisel Academy of Fine Arts. In recent years he has been pursuing trompe l'oeil painting, often retaining an element of natural history. These recent paintings have been featured in *American Artist Quarterly*, *Acrylic Highlight*, and *American Art Collector* magazines.

Statement: In 1970, on the first "Earth Day," I was young and enthusiastic about the new environmental awareness movement, and I began a career as a natural history artist, naturalist, and environmental education teacher. Society was newly dedicated to conserving wildlife and the environment, but in spite of a few notable successes since then, we have largely failed to prevent the tide of extinction. Hope springs eternal, however, and "Vanishing Circles" is hope for the flora and fauna of the Sonoran Desert. It is my hope that my paintings and those of my fellow artists will bring home a new or revitalized interest in the importance of preserving our vast natural inventory.

Kearney's bluestar
Manabu C. Saito
saitobotanicals@gmail.com

Born in Japan, Manabu Saito received a B.A. degree in industrial design from Pratt Institute in Brooklyn, after which he worked as an industrial designer for several organizations and corporations, including Sony and Nikon. In the late 1960s, Saito began painting flowers wherever he lived or traveled, especially in the Sonoran Desert and the American tropics in Surinam, Trinidad, and Costa Rica. By 1970, he'd become a fulltime botanical artist and illustrator, executing original paintings, producing limited edition prints, and illustrating books, including *Wildflowers of North America* (with more than 1,500 color illustrations). His artwork has appeared in *A Passion for Plants: Contemporary Botanical Masterworks* and in *National Geographic*, *Horticulture*, and *Audubon* magazines. In 1984, the U.S. Postal Service commissioned him to do a set of commemorative stamps depicting orchids. He has had one-man shows in such venues as the Brooklyn Botanic Garden, the New York Botanical Garden, the Horticultural Society of New York, the Arizona-Sonora Desert Museum, and the Tucson Botanical Gardens.

Statement: With a tip from a colleague, permission from the Buenos Aires National Wildlife Refuge, and the guidance of a park ranger, I found the Kearny's bluestar in Brown Canyon in April of 2001. Several plants were in full bloom along the bed of a beautiful stream. Here, I photographed them, made pencil sketches, and finally created the watercolor painting for the Vanishing Circles collection.

Arizona claret cup cactus
Constance Sayas
731 Krameria St.
Denver, Colorado 80220
720-941-5774
sayasdesign@earthlink.net

Constance Sayas is an illustrator with a degree in Fine Art and a career in the sciences. Having worked as a scientific illustrator for *Encyclopaedia Britannica* and as an exhibit designer for several major museums, she currently teaches botanical illustration at the Denver Botanic Gardens. Her award-winning botanical watercolor paintings appear in numerous collections, including the Hunt Institute of Botanical Documentation and the Brooklyn Botanic Gardens Florilegium Society.

Statement: Fascinated by the flora and fauna of the American Southwest, I was excited about the opportunity to paint the endangered Arizona claret cup cactus, and I traveled to Arizona to do extensive research, documentation, and drawing for this plant portrait. My watercolor challenge was to accurately show the numerous spines without sacrificing the painting's freshness and clarity. In the end, the greatest satisfaction came from my expanded knowledge of both paint and plant.

"Sonora Majesty" – jaguar
John Seerey-Lester
941-966-2163
seereylester@msn.com
www.Seerey-Lester.com

John Seerey-Lester began his career as a professional artist in 1974, painting historic scenes of his native England. After a trip to East Africa in 1980, he began focusing on wildlife in their natural element, and has since traveled the world to witness the wildlife he portrays. His art has been chosen for the prestigious Leigh Yawkey Woodson Art Museum's *Wildlife: An Artist's View* show and their annual *Birds in Art* show most years since he emmigrated to the United States in 1982. In 2002 and 2006, Seerey-Lester was presented with an Award of Excellence from the Society of Animal Artists. His work has been displayed in the Gilcrease Museum, among many others, and his work is in many permanent collections, including the Leigh Yawkey Woodson Art Museum, the Nature in Art Museum in England, and the White House. Seerey-Lester's art is featured in several books—most recently, *Useppa; a Passage in Time* (2006), and *Legends of the Hunt* (2010, a book he also authored).

Statement: My painting shows two jaguars—the more common spotted phase, and the rare black-coated jaguar rarely glimpsed in northern Mexico. I chose a small creek as the setting for my painting to illustrate this species' fondness for water.

western burrowing owl
Richard Sloan
janethisel@verizon.net
www.richardsloanart.com

Sadly, since this painting for Vanishing Circles was completed, Richard Sloan passed away, but his art still speaks for him. After attending the American Academy of Art in Chicago, Sloan worked as an advertising illustrator before joining that city's Lincoln Park Zoo as staff artist. In 1966, he left Lincoln Park to capture images of rain forests, soon gaining a reputation as one of the world's premiere rain forest painters. His paintings have been exhibited at the National Geographic Society's Explorers Hall, the American Museum of Natural History, Carnegie Museum, Royal Scottish Academy, Gilcrease Museum, and many other museums and galleries. His work was juried into at least 24 *Birds in Art* exhibitions at the Leigh Yawkey Woodson Art Museum, which honored Sloan as a Master Wildlife Artist. Sloan's paintings are in numerous permanent collections, including the Smithsonian Institution, Leigh Yawkey Woodson Art Museum, Arizona-Sonora Desert Museum, Arizona Wildlife Foundation, Denver Museum of Natural History, and private collections across the globe. They appear in many books, among them, *Wildlife Art / More Paintings of the Modern Masters, The Best of Wildlife Art,* and *The Raptors of Arizona,* which features 42 of his paintings.

Aravaipa Canyon, Sabino Canyon, "Along the Río Mayo" – Tropical Deciduous Forest, Sonora, Mexico
Ken Stockton
kenstockton.com

Ken Stockton's work usually depicts natural or rural landscapes of the western United States, often featuring livestock or wildlife with a special emphasis on the Sonoran and Mohave Deserts. He earned a B.S. in Landscape Architecture from the University of California, Davis, and has pursued classes in sculpting, drawing, and painting at San Bernardino Community College, Brigham Young University, and the University of Utah. He has also taken part in various plein air workshops taught by artists Matt Smith, Ray Roberts, and Phil Starke. He has participated in more than 50 exhibitions and is represented by galleries in Arizona, California, and online. His work has appeared in *Southwest Art's* "Artists to Watch" column, and twice in *Western Art Collector* previewing exhibits with his work.

Statement: My reasons for painting are really pretty simple. Painting helps me understand and savor that which I find beautiful or compelling, and provides the means of expressing it to others.

Nichol's Turk's head cactus
Lívia Vieira
liviabvs@gmail.com
55-21-2245-5584

Lívia Vieira was born in São Paulo, Brazil, and graduated in Biological Sciences from the Universidade do Estado do Rio de Janeiro (UERJ). During her botany internship, she had her first experience with scientific illustration. In 2002 she began classes with Dulce Nascimento and, in the same year, took part in the Fourth Botanical Illustration Trip in the Amazon. Two years later, she joined the Denver Botanical Gardens Botanical Art and Illustration Certificate Program, and also participated in workshops given by Jenny Phillips, Christabel King, and Pandora Sellars. She currently makes pen and ink drawings for international scientific publications. Her work regularly appears in botanical illustration exhibitions in Brazil.

Statement: As a biologist I have always been interested in the scientific approach to botanical illustration, and I always try to be as accurate as possible in my drawings. The extraordinary variety of colors and shapes in the Brazilian flora, both elegant and fantastic, will always be an important inspiration for my work.

black-footed ferret, Mt. Graham red squirrel, pronghorn
Nicholas Wilson
The Karin Newby Gallery
and Sculpture Garden
19 Tubac Rd
Tubac, AZ 85646-4217
520-398-9662
www.karinnewbygallery.com

Nicholas Wilson has been a painter, sculptor, and printmaker for more than 45 years. His animal art is in the collections of the Smithsonian Institution, National Cowboy and Western Heritage Museum in Oklahoma, Booth Western Art Museum in Georgia, Leigh Yawkey Woodson Art Museum in Wisconsin, and Arizona-Sonora Desert Museum, plus numerous corporate and private collections around the world. As a young man, Wilson was employed as Curator of Exhibits at the Desert Museum; he credits his knowledge of animal anatomy and fur texture to his frequent walks among the animal exhibits there.

Statement: When I research my subjects, I seek evidence of their existence by selecting elements for the setting. I may never actually see the animal in the wild, but I have a pretty good idea where they would be found and what they would be doing for the purpose of the painting. Getting a glimpse of the rare black-footed ferret was out of the question, though an abundance of photographic reference exists. Thanks to that, I was able to create a detailed clay model in a position of choice from which to sketch and paint. The pronghorn antelope made for an interesting scene. Here in southern Arizona, it is possible to sight herds of pronghorn in the grasslands near Sonoita. For the red squirrel, a trip to the Pinaleño Mountains is the only hope to see one.

Artworks by Artist

ARTIST	SUBJECT	PAGE
JOHN N. AGNEW	Altar Valley	117
	Desert Tortoise	11
	Gila Monster	15
	Ramsey Canyon Leopard Frog	19
EDWARD ALDRICH	Bald Eagle	47
	California Brown Pelican	51
	Ocelot	87
	Osprey	61
	Thick-billed Parrot	65
PRISCILLA BALDWIN	Black-tailed Prairie Dog	75
CAREL P. BREST VAN KEMPEN	California Condor	53
	Desert Tortoise	9
	Giant Spotted Whiptail	13
	Mexican Beaded Lizard	17
	San Esteban Chuckwalla	21
	Spotted Bat	91
BOBBIE BROWN	Bristol's Hedgehog Cactus	95
	Sabo's Pincushion Cactus	113
ADELE EARNSHAW	Violet-crowned Hummingbird	67
LARRY FANNING	Northern Aplomado Falcon	59
	Mexican Gray Wolf	83
SCOTT FRASER	Aquatic Invertebrates	43
JOE GARCIA	Abert's Towhee	45
	Masked Bobwhite	57
JANET HEATON	California Brown Pelican	50
WILLIAM HOOK	Gran Desierto de Altar/Algodone Dunes	121
	Desert Ironwood Tree	97
	Organ Pipe Cactus	107
	Sea of Cortez, Mangrove Bay	129
	Sea of Cortez	131
RACHEL IVANYI	American Crocodile	7
	Apache Trout and Gila Trout	31
	Cactus Ferruginous Pygmy Owl	49
	Desert Pupfish and Quitobaquito Pupfish	33
	Fishes of the Colorado River	35

ARTIST	SUBJECT	PAGE
RACHEL IVANYI CONT	Fish of the Gila River	37
	Fish of the Rio Yaqui	39
	Sea Turtles	23
	True Frogs	29
SHARI JONES	San Pedro River	127
LESS LULL	San Pedro River	125
JOAN MCGANN	Pima Pineapple Cactus	109
DULCE NASCIMENTO	Kearny Sumac	101
RHONDA NASS	Desert Night-blooming Cereus	99
	Pima Pineapple Cactus Flower	110
	Pima Pineapple Cactus Fruit	111
	Slender Climbing Cactus	115
ANNE PEYTON	Western Burrowing Owl	69
MARTIENA RICHTER	Margay	79
MICHAEL JAMES RIDDET	Huachuca Giant Skipper	41
	Least Bell's Vireo	55
	Merriam's Mouse	81
	Sonoran Tiger Salamander	25
	Rufous-winged Sparrow	63
	Tarahumara Frog	27
	Western Yellow-billed Cuckoo	71
MANABU C. SAITO	Kearny's Bluestar	103
CONSTANCE SAYAS	Arizona Claret Cup Cactus	93
JOHN SEEREY-LESTER	Jaguar	77
RICHARD SLOAN	Western Burrowing Owl	69
KEN STOCKTON	Aravaipa Canyon	119
	Sabino Canyon	123
	Tropical Deciduous Forest	133
LIVIA VIEIRA	Nichol's Turk's Head Cactus	105
NICHOLAS WILSON	Black-footed Ferret	73
	Mt. Graham Red Squirrel	85
	Pronghorn	89

Suggested Readings and References

Books

Aguilar, Rafaela Paredes, Thomas R. Van Devender, Richard S. Felger. *Cactáceas de Sonora, México: su Diversidad, Uso y Conservación*. Tucson: Arizona-Sonora Desert Museum Press, 2000.

Anderson, Edward F. *The Cactus Family*. Portland, Oregon: Timber Press, 2001.

Arizona Rare Plant Committee. *Arizona Rare Plant Field Guide*. Phoenix: Arizona Heritage Data Management System, Arizona Game and Fish Department, 2001.

Beattie, Heather, and Barbara Huck. *Wild West. Nature Living on the Edge: Endangered Species of Western North America*. Winnipeg: Heartland Associates, 2010.

Beck, Daniel D. *Biology of Gila Monsters and Beaded Lizards*. Berkeley: University of California Press, 2005.

Brusca, Richard C. (ed.). *The Gulf of California: Biodiversity and Conservation*. Arizona-Sonora Desert Museum Studies in Natural History. Tucson: UA Press and ASDM Press, 2010.

Brusca, Richard C., Erin Kimrey, and Wendy Moore. *Seashore Guide to the Northern Gulf of California*. Tucson: ASDM Press, 2004.

Brown, David E. (ed.). *The Wolf in the Southwest: The Making of an Endangered Species*. Tucson: UA Press, 1983.

Cartron, Jean-Luc, Gerardo Ceballos, and Richard Stephen Felger (eds.). *Biodiversity, Ecosystms, and Conservation in Northern Mexico*. New York: Oxford University Press, 2005.

Ehrlich, Paul R., David S. Dobkin. *Birds in Jeopardy: the Imperiled and Extinct Birds of the United States and Canada, Including Hawaii and Puerto Rico*. Stanford, California: Stanford University Press, 1992.

Felger, Richard Stephen. *Flora of the Gran Desierto and Río Colorado of Northwestern Mexico*. Tucson: UA Press, 2000.

Felger, Richard Stephen, and Bill Broyles, (eds.). *Dry Borders: Great Natural Reserves of the Sonoran Desert*. Salt Lake City: University of Utah, 2006.

Ghelbach, Frederick R. *Mountain Islands and Desert Seas: A Natural History of the U.S.-Mexican Borderlands*. College Station, Texas: A&M Press, 1981.

Glinski, Richard L. *The Raptors of Arizona*. Tucson: UA Press and Arizona Game and Fish Department, 1998.

Hadley, Diana, Peter Warshall, and Don Bufkin. *Environmental Change in Aravaipa 1870-1970: An Ethnoecological Survey*. Cultural Resource Series No. 7. Prepared by Hadley Associates. Phoenix, Arizona: Arizona State Office of the Bureau of Land Management, 1991.

Hall, E. Raymond. *The Mammals of North America*, Vols. I & II. NY, NY: John Wiley & Sons, 1981.

Hassler, Lynn. *Hummingbirds of the American West*. Tucson: Rio Nuevo, 2002.

Johnsgard, Paul A. *The Hummingbirds of North America*. Washington, D.C.: Smithsonian Institution Press, 1983.

Lazaroff, David W. *Sabino Canyon: The Life of a Southwestern Oasis*. Tucson and London: UA Press, 1993.

Lowe, Charles H., Cecil R. Schwalbe, Terry B. Johnson. *The Venomous Reptiles of Arizona*. Phoenix: Arizona Game and Fish Department, 1986.

Matthews, John R., and David W. Lowe. *The Official World Wildlife Fund Guide to Endangered Species of North America*. Volume 1. Plants, Mammals. Volume 2. Birds, Reptiles, Amphibians, Fishes, Mussels, Crustaceans, Snails, Insects, and Arachnids. Washington, D.C.: Beacham Publications, Inc., 1990.

Nabhan, Gary, Richard C. Brusca, and Louella Holter (eds.). *Conserving Migratory Pollinators and Nectar Corridors in Western North America*. Arizona-Sonora Desert Museum Studies in Natural History. Tucson: UA Press and ASDM Press, 2004.

North American Bird Conservation Initiative, U.S. Committee. *The State of the Birds, United States of America, 2009*. Washington, D.C.: U.S. Dept. of Interior, 2009.

Phillips, Allan, Joe Marshall, and Gale Monson. *The Birds of Arizona*. Tucson: UA Press, 1964, 1978.

Phillips, Steven J., and Patricia Wentworth Comus (eds.). *A Natural History of the Sonoran Desert*. Berkeley: University of California Press; and Tucson: ASDM Press, 2000.

Robichaux, Robert H., and David A. Yetman (eds.). *The Tropical Deciduous Forest of Alamos: Biodiversity of a Threatened Ecosystem in Mexico*, Tucson: UA Press, 2000.

Stebbins, Robert C., and Nathan W. Cohen. *A Natural History of Amphibians*. Princeton, New Jersey: Princeton University Press, 1995.

Steinbeck, John and Edward F. Ricketts. *The Sea of Cortez: A Leisurely Journal of Travel and Research*. New York: Viking Press, 1941 [reprinted 2009 by Penguin Books]

Taylor, Nigel P. *The Genus Echinocereus*. Portland, Oregon: The Royal Botanic Gardens, Kew, in association with Timber Press, 1985.

Tobin, Mitch. *Endangered: Biodiversity on the Brink*. Golden, Colorado: Fulcrum Publishing, 2010.

Turner, Raymond M., Janice E. Bowers, and Tony L. Burgess. *Sonoran Desert Plants: An Ecological Atlas*. Tucson: UA Press, 1995

Wilson, Don E., and Sue Ruff (eds.). *The Smithsonian Book of North American Mammals*. Washington, D.C: Smithsonian Institution Press, 1999.

Yetman, David A. *The Organ Pipe Cactus*. Tucson: UA Press, 2006.

Journals

sonorensis, *Jaguar* Vol. 28 (1). Tucson: Arizona-Sonora Desert Museum Press, 2008.

sonorensis, *The Sea of Cortez* Vol. 22 (1). Tucson: Arizona-Sonora Desert Museum Press, 2002.

Online websites

Arizona Game and Fish Department. *http://www.azgfd.gov/* Heritage Data Management System.

Arizona-Sonora Desert Museum. *http://www.desertmuseum.org/*

Bat Conservation International. *http://www.batcon.org/*

Black-footed Ferret Recovery Implementation Team. *http://www.blackfootedferret.org/*

Bureau of Land Management. *http://www.blm.gov/*

Center for Biologial Diversity. *http://www.biologicaldiversity.org/*

Cornell Lab of Ornithology. *The Birds of North America Online* at *http://bna.birds.cornell.edu/bna/species/*

CPC National Collection Plant Profile. *http://www.centerforplantconservation.org*

Defenders of Wildlife. *http://defenders.org/wildlife/*

National Audubon Society. *http://www.audubon.org/*

National Park Service. *http://www.nps.gov/index.htm*

National Wildlife Federation. *http://www.nwf.org/Wildlife/Wildlife-Library/*

NatureServe Explorer: An Online Encyclopedia of Life. *http://natureserve.org.explorer/*

Pima County. Sonoran Desert Conservation Plan. *http://www.pima.gov/CMO/SDCP/species/fsheets/*

The Encyclopedia of Earth. *http://www.eoearth.org/*

The Nature Conservancy. *http://www.nature.org/*

U.S. Fish and Wildlife Service. *http://www.fws.gov/*

U.S. Forest Service. *http://www.fs.fed.us/*

U.S. Geological Survey. *http://www.usgs.gov/*

Common and Scientific Names for Species in Narratives
Common Name *(Scientific Name)*

Abert's squirrel *(Sciurus aberti)*
American bullfrog *(Lithobates catesbeianus)*
Arizona sycamore *(Platanus wrightii)*
Arizona walnut *(Juglans major)*
banner-tailed kangaroo rat *(Dipodomys spectabilis)*
barn owl *(Tyto alba)*
barred tiger salamander *(Ambystoma mavortium mavortium)*
beargrass *(Nolina microcarpa)*
beaver *(Castor* spp.*)*
Bell's vireo *(Vireo bellii)*
belted kingfisher *(Megaceryle alcyon)*
Bermuda grass *(Cynodon dactylon)*
big galleta *(Pleuraphis rigida)*
bighorn sheep *(Ovis canadensis nelsoni)*
black bear *(Ursus americanus)*
black-hawk *(Buteogallus anthracinus)*
black-throated magpie jay *(Calocitta colliei)*
black-throated sparrow *(Amphispiza bilineata)*.
bluntheaded tree snake *(Imantodes* spp.*)*
bobcat *(Lynx rufus)*
Brasil tree *(Haematoxylum brasiletto)*
Brewer's sparrow *(Spizella breweri)*
brook trout *(Salvelinus fontinalis)*
brown booby *(Sula leucogaster)*
brown trout *(Salmo trutta)*
buffelgrass *(Pennisetum ciliare)*
bullfrog *(Lithobates catesbelana)*
bursage *(Ambrosia* spp.*)*
California boxthorn *(Lycium californicum)*
cardinal flower *(lobelia cardinalis)*
cat claw acacia *(Acacia greggii)*
chipping sparrow *(Spizella passerina)*
cholla cactus *(Opuntia* spp.*)*
clouded anole *(Anolis nebulosus)*
clouded leopard *(Neofelis nebulosa)*
coatimundi *(Nasua nasua)*
common carp *(Cyprinus carpio)*
common chuckwalla *(Sauromalus obesus)*
Cooper's hawk *(Accipiter cooperii)*
coral bean tree *(Erythrina flabelliformis)*
corvina *(Cynoscion* spp.*)*
cottonwood, or Freemont cottonwood *(Populus fremontii)*
cowbird *(Molothrus ater)*

coyote *(Canis latrans)*
crane hawk *(Geranospiza caerulescens)*
creosotebush or creosote *(Larrea tridentata)*
crested caracara *(Polyborus plancus)*
cuajilote *(Pseudobombax palmeri)*
cutthroat trout *(Oncorhynchus clarkii)*
desert cotton *(Gossypium thurberi)*
desert sucker *(Catostomus clarki)*
desert spoon *(Dasylirion wheeleri)*
dune evening primrose *(Oenothera deltoides)*
eastern yellow-billed cuckoo *(Coccyzus americanus americanus)*
elegant tern *(Sterna elegans)*
elegant trogon *(Trogon elegans)*
elephant trees *(Bursera* spp.*)*
ferruginous hawk *(Buteo regalis)*
fountaingrass *(Pennisetum setaceum)*
fringe-toed lizard *(Uma rufopunctata)*
garter snake *(Thamnophis sirtalis)*
gazelle *(Gazella* spp.*)*
giant brown sea cucumber *(Parastichopus fuscus)*
giant squids *(Architeuthis* spp.*)*
Goodding willow *(Salix gooddingii)*
gopher snake *(Pituophis melanoleucus)*
gray fox *(Urocyon cinereoargenteus)*
gray hawk *(Asturina nitida)*
gray wolf *(Canis lupus)*
great horned owl *(Bubo virginianus)*
green kingfisher *(Chloroceryle americana)*
green sunfish *(Lepomus cyanellus)*
grizzly bear *(Ursus arctos horribilis)*
guayacan tree *(Guaiacum coulteri)*
Gunnison prairie dog *(Cynomys gunnisoni)*
hackberry *(Celtis* spp.*)*
house mouse *(Mus musculus)*
horn shark *(Heterodontus francisci)*
Huachuca agave *(Agave parryi* var. *huachucensis)*
indigo snake *(Drymarchon corais)*
javelina *(Tayassu tajacu)*
kapok tree *(Ceiba pentandra)*
kit fox *(Vulpes macrotis)*
largemouth bass *(Micropterus salmoides)*
lazuli bunting *(Passerina amoena)*
least tern *(Sternula antillarum)*

Lehmann lovegrass (*Eragrostis lehmanniana*)
lesser long-nosed bat (*Leptonycteris curasoae*)
lilac-crowned parrot (*Amazona finschi*)
longfin dace (*Agosia chrysogaster*)
mesquite (*Prosopis* spp.)
Mexican blue oak (*Quercus oblongifolia*)
Mexican spotted owl (*Strix occidentalis lucida*)
military macaws (*Ara militaris*)
monkey flowers (*Mimulus* spp.)
Montezuma bald cypress (*Taxodium mucronatum* var. *mexicanum*)
mosquitofish (*Gambusia affinis*)
mountain lion (*Puma concolor*)
mountain mahogany (*Cercocarpus montanus*)
mountain plover (*Charadrius montanus*)
mourning dove (*Zenaida macroura*)
mule deer (*Odocoileus hemionus*)
nine-banded armadillo (*Dasypus novemcinctus*)
northern beardless-tyrannulet (*Camptostoma imberbe*)
northern goshawk (*Accipiter gentilis*)
ocotillo (*Fouquieria splendens*)
oreganillo (*Aloysia wrightii*)
palo verdes (*Parkinsonia* spp.)
Peirson's milk-vetch (*Astragalus magdalenae* var. *peirsonii*)
pelicans (*Pelicanus* spp.)
pink sand verbena (*Abronia umbellata*)
pink-trumpet tree (*Tabebuia impetiginosa*)
point-leaf manzanita (*Arctostaphylos pungens*)
prairie dogs (*Cynomys* spp.)
queen butterfly (*Danaus gilippus*)
raccoon (*Procyon lotor*)
rainbow trout (*Oncorhynchus mykiss*)
red brome (*Bromus rubens*)
red shiner (*Cyprinella lutrensis*)
red-tailed hawk (*Buteo jamaicensis*)
regal ringneck snake (*Diadophis punctatus regalis*)
ringtail (*Bassariscus astutus*)
river otter (*Lontra longicaudis*)
rock fig (*Ficus petiolaris*)
rock hibiscus (*Hibiscus denudatus*)
Russian thistle, or tumbleweed (*Salsola kali*)
sacaton (*Sporobolus wrightii*)
saguaro (*Carnegiea gigantea*)
salt cedars (*Tamarix* spp.)

sand food (*Pholisma sonorae*)
sharp-shinned hawk (*Accipiter striatus*)
shovel-nosed sand snake (*Chionactis occipitalis*)
silverbush (*Ditaxis lanceolata*)
Sinaloan white-tailed deer (*Odocoileus virginianus sinaloae*)
six weeks grama (*Bouteloua barbata*)
six weeks threeawn (*Aristida adscensionis*)
Sonoran box turtle (*Terrapene klauberi*)
Sonoran Desert fringe-toed lizard (*Uma notata*)
southwestern willow flycatchers (*Empidonax traillii extimus*)
speckled dace (*Rhinichthys osculus*)
spectacle-pod (*Dimorphocarpa pinnatifida*)
sperm whale (*Physeter macrocephalus*)
spiny chuckwalla (*Sauromalus hispidus*)
spotted owl (*Strix occidentalis*)
squawbush (*Rhus trilobata*)
stinkbugs (*Chlorchroa ligata*)
swift fox (*Vulpes velox*)
swordfish (*Xiphias gladius*)
tamarisk (*Tamarix* spp.)
tepeguaje (*Lysiloma watsonii*)
totoaba (*Totoaba macdonaldi*)
tree morning glory (*Ipomoea arborescens*)
trixis (*Trixis californica*)
turpentine bush (*Ericameria laricifolia*)
vaquita (*Phoecina sinus*)
velvet mesquite (*Prosopis velutina*)
vermilion flycatcher (*Pyrocephalus rubinus*)
western ornate box turtle (*Terrapene ornata*)
western mosquitofish (*Gambusia affinis*)
western pipistrelle bat (*Pipistrellus hesperus*)
western screech owl (*Megascops kennicottii*)
western scrub-jay (*Aphelocoma californica*)
whiteball acacia tree (*Acacia angustissima*)
white-tailed deer (*Odocoileus virginianus*)
willow (*Salix* spp.)
wolfberry (*Lycium* spp.)
yellow bullhead (*Ameiurus natalis*)
zauschneria (*Epilobium canum*)

Agencies Designating Species Conservation Status

As the U.S. Fish and Wildlife Service points out, the U.S. Congress recognized endangered and threatened species as having "esthetic, ecological, historical, recreational, and scientific value to the Nation and its people" when it passed the Endangered Species Act (ESA). Ecosystem services like the capture, filtration, and storage of water; the production of the oxygen we breath; the pollination of countless fruits and vegetables; and the creation and maintenance of topsoil in which they grow—these are just a few of the services to our society afforded by healthy ecosystems, ecosystems in which biodiversity plays the leading, sustaining role.

Under the ESA "endangered" refers to a species in danger of extinction throughout all or a significant portion of its range. "Threatened" means a species is likely to become endangered within the foreseeable future. For the purposes of the ESA, Congress defined species to include "subspecies, varieties, and for vertebrates, distinct population segments." A species may be deemed "critically endangered" or simply "endangered."

The following agencies or organizations list, evaluate, or oversee the conservation status of wildlife species within their purview.

United States Endangered Species Act
www.fws.gov/endangered/
www.nmfs.noaa.gov/pr/laws/esa

The number and species listed as endangered or threatened under the Endangered Species Act (ESA) is always changing, as populations of species recover or slip further toward extinction. The U.S. Fish and Wildlife Service (FWS) and the National Marine Fishers Service (NMFS) evaluate candidates and administer the list (NOAA currently oversees about 70 listed marine species). A summary of listed species is updated regularly at the websites above. As of August 1, 2010, there was a total of 1,375 species listed as "endangered" or "threatened" under the ESA in the United States (1,950 including foreign lands or waters). These numbers represent only species formally listed as threatened or endangered, but not all qualified species are actually listed due to various bureaucratic or political concerns. Many species at risk never become candidates.

IUCN
International Union for the Conservation of Nature
www.icun.org

The IUCN maintains a conservation status listing call the Red List. According to the IUCN, rated species (with sufficient data available) fall into one of 7 categories from "extinct" to "least concern," including "endangered" and "threatened." ICUN definitions vary slightly in meaning from the "threatened" and "endangered" definitions of the U.S. Endangered Species Act. The ICUN website provides more detail on status definition.

CITES
Convention on International Trade in Endangered Species of Wild Fauna and Flora
www.cites.org

Also known as the "Washington Convention," this voluntary agreement was initially signed by 80 governments (effective 1973) to prevent international trade of wild animals or plants that would endanger the survival of the species. The list now includes close to 33,000 species. CITES protection measures often involve quotas or prohibition of trade. More than 175 countries have now signed onto the convention, but not all those countries have laws or means to enforce the protection measures. Details are provided at the CITES website.

Arizona Game and Fish Department (AZGFD)
Nongame and Endangered Wildlife Program
www.azgfd.gov/w_c/nongame_species.shtml

The primary purpose of this program is to "protect, restore, preserve, and maintain nongame and endangered wildlife as part of the natural diversity of Arizona." The AZGFD lists tiers of "Species of Greatest Conservation Need" following the ESA Endangered Species List, as well as species with candidate status for the list and those deemed "sensitive species" by the U.S. Bureau of Land Management or the U.S. Forest Service. The AZGFD oversees permits for collection or management and recovery programs for these species. Sensitive species are species that could become endangered or extirpated from a state or within a significant portion of its range in the foreseeable future, or those under review for federal listing.

SEMARNAT
Secretaría de Medio Ambiente y Recursos Naturales
(The Ministry of Environment and Natural Resources)
www.semarnat.gob.mx/

This agency of the Mexican government oversees standards for the preservation and restoration of natural ecosystems and for the sustainable use of flora and fauna, among many other components of the environment (e.g. water and other resources). It monitors the enforcement of environmental laws and it inventories wildlife populations in cooperation with state and local agencies and institutions. It also regulates the trade or transit of wild species. Its SNIARN (National Information System for Environmental and Natural Resources, which includes databases with statistics, maps, graphs, etc.) is accessible to the public through a portal on its website.

Glossary

accipiter – a bird of prey in the genus *Accipiter*.

algae – a group of protists (non-animal, non-plant) that use photosynthesis to produce complex organic compounds; species in this group range from single-celled to many-celled (e.g. seaweed).

alluvial soils – loose soils eroded from a slope and deposited by running water.

anther – a pollen-bearing portion of the stamen of a flower.

anthropogenic – influenced or caused by humans.

apex predator – a predator at the top of the food chain.

arboreal – relating to trees; living in trees.

areole – in cactus, a small protrusion that produces felt, spines, and new growth.

Arizona Upland – the northeastern section, the highest and coldest subdivision, of the Sonoran Desert, containing numerous mountain ranges. Trees are common on rocky slopes as well as drainages, and saguaros are found everywhere but on the valley floors. This community is also called the saguaro-palo verde forest. It is the only subdivision that experiences frequent hard winter frosts.

bajada – an "apron" of land across the front of a mountain range created from multiple alluvial deposits over time

bivalve – a class of molluscs in which the body is encased within two shells, or "valves."

brackish water – naturally-occurring water that is salty, but less salty than seawater.

brood parasitism – in birds, a competitive strategy in which one bird lays an egg among the eggs of another bird, where the hatchling is reared by the nonparent, host bird.

bycatch – the aggregate nontarget species caught in fishing which are, typically, subsequently destroyed or discarded.

canopy – in forests, a collective term for the crowns of the trees or tree tops; the uppermost vegetative layer of the forest.

captive breeding program – a program in which individuals of a species are bred and reared, typically as a source of new individuals for reintroduction into their natural habitat; most captive breeding or rearing programs are maintained by zoos or wildlife agencies and organizations.

carrion – a carcass of a dead animal.

chaparral – a semiarid biome that occurs on the west coast of every continent between about 30° and 40° north latitude, unique in its mild, moist winters and hot, dry summers; mature chaparral consists almost solely of woody evergreen shrubs with small leathery leaves.

chlorophyll – any of several green pigments associated with chloroplasts, or with certain bacterial membranes, responsible for trapping light energy for photosynthesis.

ciénega – a southwestern U.S. and Spanish term referring to a swamp or marsh, especially those fed by springs

cloaca – the common opening of intestinal, reproductive, and urinary tracts in some animal species (e.g., birds, lizards)

composite – of plants, a member of the Asteraceae family; many species in this family bear individual flowers in a disc head that appears to be a single flower (e.g. daisy).

conifer – an evergreen cone-bearing tree or shrub with needlelike leaves.

coniferous forest – a forest dominated by cone-bearing trees, especially pines, firs, and spruces in the Northern Hemisphere.

cosmopolitan species – a species found in many places around the world.

crepuscular – (zool.) active in the dim twilight of dusk or dawn.

critical habitat – an area essential to the survival and conservation of a species, especially those listed on the U.S. endangered species list.

crustacean – an arthropod in the subphylum Crustacea, having segmented bodies and hard exoskeletons (e.g. crabs, shrimps, lobsters).

DDT – dichlorodiphenyltrichloroethane, a synthetic pesticide used heavily as an agricultural pesticide after World War II, banned in the United States in 1972.

deciduous trees – trees that drop their leaves (or entire branches) seasonally, remaining leafless part of the year.

depredation – damage or loss.

desert – Earth's driest biome, with vegetation determined by the extreme aridity; desert vegetation around the world looks more or less similar, with most plants widely spaced and having small or absent leaves.

desert scrub – a landscape with numerous woody species (e.g., palo verdes, mesquites, ironwood), cacti, and a suite of other succulents or plants that behave like succulents (e.g., yuccas, ocotillo). These plants grow widely spaced because they rely on extensive, shallow root systems adapted to making use of infrequent and little rainfall; native annual herbs occasionally grow in profusion in these "empty" spaces. The vegetative community of **Sonoran Desert scrub** is characterized by saguaro and cholla cacti, and palo verde, creosote, and mesquite.

detritus – (biol.) small particles of organic material, often dead plants or animals and/or fecal matter.

diurnal – active during daylight hours.
echolocation – a natural biological sonar system used by many species of bats, by shrews, and by most cetaceans (e.g. dolphins and whales); a system that uses echoes from vocal emissions to locate and identify objects.
ecologist – a person who studies ecology, or the interrelationships among plants, animals, and their physical environments.
ecosystem – a community of plants, animals, and microorganisms that are linked by energy and nutrient flows and that interact with each other and with the physical environment (e.g. rainforests, deserts, coral reefs, grasslands, and rotting saguaro cactus).
ectotherms – animals that regulate their body temperature by use of their surroundings (e.g., sun, warm rocks, shade, cool rocks).
endangered species – a species in danger of imminent extinction; in the United States, use of this term implies an official listing under the Endangered Species Act.
endemic – native to, and naturally restricted to, one specific region.
epiphyte – a type of plant, sometimes called an "air plant," that anchors itself by its roots to a tree or rock, and that absorbs nutrients mainly from air and water through its leaves.
eradication – thorough extermination.
esteros – coastal or tidal lagoons with moderately hypersaline water.
evapotranspiration – of plants, the emission of water by the opening and closing of stomata in leaves, which helps regulate leaf temperature.
evolution – change over time in the populations of individual organisms differing genetically in one or more traits; descent with modification.
evolve – to undergo the process of evolution.
exotic vegetation – vegetation not native to the habitat, country, or continent in which it is found.
extant – currently existing; not destroyed or lost.
extinction – the termination of a species (or any other taxon) by natural or anthropogenic means; species have: (1) an origin (speciation), (2) a life-span (anagenesis), and (3) an end (extinction).
extirpation – complete disappearance within a specific area; i.e., a species or subspecies disappearing from a locality or region without becoming extinct throughout its entire range.
fauna – the animals found in a given area.
flora – the plants found in a given area.

forbs – herbaceous flowering plants.
fragmentation – (ecol.) the breaking up of large habitats into smaller, isolated areas—one of the main forms of habitat degradation and a primary reason species become threatened with extinction and that global biodiversity is in decline.
gallery forest – a corridor of trees, typically along rivers, that stand out in a landscape otherwise not heavily treed (e.g. deserts or grasslands).
grassland – a semi-arid biome characterized by warm, humid summers with moderate rain and cold, dry winters (the winter-rainfall grassland of the central valley of California excepted); grass is the dominant life form, while scores of species form a continuous cover over large areas, with few trees and many annuals.
habitat – the place or environment where a plant or animal naturally lives and grows; a group of particular environmental conditions.
halophytic plants – salt-tolerant plants that grow in salty or alkaline soils or habitats.
herb – (botan.) a seed-producing plant that does not produce woody tissues, the stems of which usually die back at the end of a growing season (but which, in some species, resprout from the root in following seasons).
herbivore – an animal that eats mainly plants.
herpetologist – a person who studies amphibians or reptiles.
hibernation – (zool.) a period of dormancy or inactivity in response to cold or drought, during which metabolic processes are significantly reduced and body temperatures may be greatly lowered.
Holocene Epoch – geologic period from present day to about 12,000 years ago.
horticulture – the industry, science, or art of cultivating ornamental plants, fruits, or vegetables.
hybrid – (biol.) an individual formed by mating between unlike forms, usually genetically differentiated populations, races, or species.
hybridize – to produce hybrids by the mating of unlike forms.
invasive species – an aggressive species, usually not a native, that displaces other species—most commonly a naturalized species occupying a disturbed habitat, although the most destructive invasives also displace natives in intact communities.
invertebrates – animals lacking backbones (i.e., vertebral columns).

larva – the early (immature) life history stage of many invertebrates, amphibians, and fishes that is unlike its adult form and must metamorphose before assuming adult characteristics (pl., larvae).

larval host plant – a species of plant upon which a given species of animal (e.g. moths and butterflies) depends to provide food or housing for its larvae.

legume – a member of the pea family; plants that have seed pods that split along two sides.

Madrean evergreen woodland – a forested community dominated by evergreen oaks (but also containing junipers and pine trees) and characterized by mild winters, and warm wet summers; a warm-temperate community of the Sierra Madre Occidental extending as far north as central Arizona.

mangroves – an informal classification of certain trees and shrubs that grow in a zone between high and low tides; important in stabilizing coastal land and serving as breeding grounds for birds, molluscs, and fish.

metamorphose – to go through the process of metamorphosis.

metamorphosis – in animals, a radical change occurring between one developmental or life history stage and another (e.g. the metamorphosis from a larval to an adult form).

midden – a refuse heap piled by animals or humans; also, a dunghill or dungheap.

monsoon – a dramatic seasonal shift in winds that brings summer rains.

nectar – a liquid containing sugars that is produced by flowers or other plant parts.

Neotropical – occurring in or characteristic of the tropics of the New World (south, east, and west from the central plateau of Mexico, including tropical Central and South America).

Neotropical migrant – species that migrate seasonally from the New World tropics to North America to nest.

neurotoxin – a poisonous substance produced by a living organism that, when introduced into animal tissues, acts on the nervous system.

nocturnal – active at night.

nonnative species – a species that naturally occurs in one region but has arrived in another region (usually by human activity), where it would not naturally have migrated because of some barrier, such as an ocean; also referred to as "introduced species," "exotic species," or "alien species."

obligate – capable of surviving only in a specific set of conditions (e.g. a specific habitat, substrate, or other environmental condition).

old-growth forest – a forest in near pristine condition containing large trees well past maturity, hundreds or sometimes thousands of years old, making up a community with unique ecological features.

Oligocene Epoch – geologic period from about 33.7 to 3.8 million years ago, part of the Tertiary Period.

omnivore – an organism that eats both animal and plant materials.

omnivorous – eating both animal and plant materials.

perennial – a term describing a plant that lives from year to year (as opposed to an annual, which lives for only a year or less).

permeable – having pores or openings through which liquids or gases can pass.

piscivore – an organism that eats fishes.

plankton – microscopic aquatic animals and algae.

Pleistocene Epoch – geologic period from about 2,588 million years ago to 12,000 years ago.

poach – to take a plant or animal illegally.

pollinate – in plants, to transfer pollen from the anther to the receptive surface (stigma) of the ovary of flowers, an essential step in the production of the fruit.

polyp – in cnidarians, the sessile, typically asexual stage in the life cycle of a species; **colonial polyps** (e.g. corals) are groups of polyps connected and functioning together.

pubescent – covered with soft, short hairs; velvety.

pupa – the nonfeeding, nonmobile stage between the last larval stage and the adult stage in holometabolous insects—the stage in which cellular metamorphosis takes place as latent genes turn on and obsolete genes are turned off, during which time the insect undergoes dramatic anatomical changes.

pupate – to pass through a pupal stage.

raptors – birds that eat live prey and also have excellent vision, sharp talons, and hooked or curved beaks.

reintroduction – the release or planting of species into the wild from a captive population or from another location where the species survives naturally.

riparian area – an area influenced by surface or subsurface water flows, evidenced by facultative or obligate wetland plant species.

riparian forest – a forest growing alongside a watercourse or wetland.

semi-desert grassland – a grassland intermediate between the true prairies of the American Midwest and deserts. Compared with prairie grassland, the grasses in desert grassland are shorter, less dense, and are more frequently interspersed with desert shrubs and succulents.

sky islands – high mountain ranges isolated from each other by intervening basins of desert and grassland or other disparate ecosystems that are barriers to the free movement of woodland and forest species from higher elevations, in much the same way seas isolate species on oceanic islands.

species – a group of individuals that naturally (or potentially) interbreed in the wild to produce fertile offspring and are thus on an evolutionary trajectory separate from those of other species, typically recognizable by a unique set of characteristics that distinguishes them from other species.

stamen – in plants, a male (pollen-producing) unit of a flower, usually composed of an anther, which bears the pollen, and a filament, which is a stalk supporting the anther.

stigma – in plants, the receptive part of the pistil (the female reproductive part of a flower) on which the pollen is deposited, generally situated at the top or tip of the pistil.

stomata – the gas-exchange pores in the epidermis of a plant (*aka* stomates).

subspecies – a named geographic race or group of populations of a species that share one or more distinctive features and occupies a distinct geographic area.

succulent – plants, such as cactuses and euphorbias, that have fleshy tissues that store and conserve moisture

tableland – a wide, level, elevated expanse of land; a plateau.

tectonic plates – large sections of the lithosphere (upper layer of the Earth) that move in relation to one another; on Earth there are now 7 or 8 major plates and many minor plates.

temperate deciduous forest – forest characterized by dense stands of broadleaf trees that drop their foliage in winter, with herbaceous perennials well-represented, along with the trees and shrubs. In the Sonoran Desert Region, this biome is represented by scattered aspen groves and ribbons of riparian trees.

Tertiary Period – geologic period from about 1.8 to 65 million years ago.

thornscrub – a biome in which vegetation consists largely of short trees, ten to twenty feet tall, and shrubs, with cacti also common in the New World communities; generally denser and taller than desert vegetation, with many thorny species, annuals and herbaceous perennials abundant and vines well represented.

torpor – a state of dormancy or inactivity.

Triassic Period – geologic period from about 250 to 200 million years ago.

tropical forest – a forest biome dictated by the absence of freezing temperatures and the occurrence of ample rainfall for at least part of the year. Some tropical forests have a dry season, while tropical rain forest is never stressed for water. **Tropical deciduous forests** have a dry season lasting from three to nine months, during which time many of the plants become deciduous.

tundra – the most poleward and highest-elevation biome, characterized by extremely cold winters and with ground-hugging woody shrubs and perennial herbs as the dominant plant life forms.

vertebrate – an animal whose nerve cord is enclosed in a backbone of bony units called vertebrae; members of the chordate subphylum Vertebrata (e.g., fishes, amphibians, reptiles, birds, mammals).

viability – of species, the ability to exist and develop.

viable population – a population of a species large enough and healthy enough to continue to thrive in the wild.

water table – the uppermost surface of natural groundwater, below which the subsurface material is saturated; the top of the groundwater aquifer.

watershed – an area of land where all of the surface and subsurface water drains to the same place; an area sharing a hydrolic system.

wetland – an area of low-lying land permanently or periodically submerged or inundated by fresh or saline water (e.g. lakes, rivers, estuaries, marshes, bogs).

Index

Abert's squirrel (*Sciurus aberti*) 84
Abert's towhee (*Pupil aberti*) 44, 116
ahuehuete (aka Montezuma bald cypress) 132
Alamos, Sonora 132
Algodones Dunes 120
Altar Valley 48, 56, 116
Altar Wash 116
Amathusia venerid (*Chionopsis amathusia*) 42
American crocodile (*Crocodylus acutus*) 6, 130
Annette's cowrie (*Cypraea annettae*) 42
Apache National Forest 82
Apache trout (*Oncorhynchus apache*) 30
apex predator 46, 82
aquaculture 106
Aravaipa Canyon 118
Arizona claret cup cactus (*Echinocereus arizonicus*) 92, 94
Arizona Forest Reserve 122
Arizona Game and Fish Department 16, 80, 157
Arizona sycamore (*Platanus wrightii*) 66
Arizona walnut (*Juglans major*) 102, 118
Arizona-Sonora Desert Museum 20, 26, 82, 102, 108, 132, 136
Arizona Upland 16, 96
bald eagle (*Haliaeetus leucocephalus*) 46, 76
banner-tailed kangaroo rats (*Dipodomys spectabilis*) 68
barn owl (*Tyto alba*) 48
bats 68, 76, 90, 106, 122, 128, 137
beargrass (*Nolina microcarpa*) 92
beautiful shiner (*Cyprinella formosa*) 38
beaver (*Castor* spp.) 36, 118, 124, 126
Bell's vireo (*Vireo bellii*) 54, 116
belted kingfisher (*Megaceryle alcyon*) 118, 122
Bering Land Bridge 72
Bermuda grass (*Cynodon dactylon*) 122
berrendo 88
bighorn sheep (*Ovis canadensis nelsoni*) 118
Birds of Arizona 56, 60, 64
black bear (*Ursus americanus*) 18, 118
black murcx (*Chicoreus nigritus*) 42
Black River 42
black hawk (*Buteogallus anthracinus*) 118

black sea turtle (*Chelonia mydas*) 22
black-footed ferret (*Mustela nigripes*) 72, 74
black-skinned Panamic whelk (*Pleuroploca granosa*) 42
black-tailed prairie dogs (*Cynomys ludovicianus*) 58, 74
black-throated magpie jay (*Calocitta colliei*) 132
black-throated sparrow (*Amphispiza bilineata*) 62
blunt-headed tree snake (*Imantodes* spp.) 132
bobcat (*Lynx rufus*) 84, 122
bonytail chub (*Gila elegans*) 34
border fence 76, 86, 88
bottom-trawling 130
box turtles,
    western ornate (*Terrapene ornata*) 118
    Sonoran (*Terrapene klauberi*) 124
Brasil tree (*Haematoxylum brasiletto*) 132
Brewer's sparrow (*Spizella breweri*) 62
Bristol's hedgehog cactus (*Echinocereus bristolii*) 94
Buenos Aires National Wildlife Refuge 56, 116
buffelgrass (*Pennisetum ciliare*) 48, 96, 104
bullfrog (*Lithobates catesbelana*) 24, 26, 28, 38
Bureau of Land Management 12, 118, 126, 136, 157
bursage (*Ambrosia* spp.) 88, 96
bycatch 22, 158
Cabeza Prieta Mountains 100
cactus ferruginous pygmy owl (*Glaucidium brasilianum cactorum*) 48, 116
California boxthorn (*Lycium californicum*) 114
California brown pelican (*Pelicanus occidentalis californicus*) 50, 116
California condor (*Gymnogyps californianus*) 52
California floater (*Anodonta californiensis*) 42
canine distemper 72
cardinal flower (*lobelia cardinalis*) 118
carrion 46, 52, 76
cat claw acacia (*Acacia greggii*) 102
catfish 34, 36, 38
cattle 24, 44, 74, 76
    trampling 38, 94
    country 126,
    tanks 24, 28

chaparral 86
chestnut cowrie (*Cypraea spadicea*) 42
chipping sparrow (*Spizella passerina*) 62
Chiricahua leopard frog (*Lithobates chiricahuensis*) 18, 28
chitons 42
chytridiomycosis 18, 26, 28
ciénega 24, 28, 32, 36, 38, 116, 124
Cienega Creek 80
CITES 6, 20, 156
clams, freshwater 42
climate change 5, 30, 88
clouded anole (*Anolis nebulosus*) 132
clouded leopard (*Neofelis nebulosa*) 78
coatimundi (*Nasua nasua*) 118
Colorado pikeminnow (*Ptychocheilus lucius*) 34
Colorado River 28, 34, 50, 120, 137
Comca'ac (i.e., Seri People) 20, 106
common carp (*Cyprinus carpio*) 124
Cooper's hawk (*Accipiter cooperii*) 54, 84
coral bean tree (*Erythrina flabelliformis*) 132
corvina (*Cynoscion* spp.) 130
cottonwood or Freemont cottonwood (*Populus fremontii*) 12, 36, 48, 70, 118, 122, 124
cowbirds 44, 54
cowries 42
coyote (*Canis latrans*) 10, 54, 56, 68, 72, 74, 86, 88
crane hawk (*Geranospiza caerulescens*) 132
crayfish 24, 34, 122
creosote or creosotebush (*Larrea tridentata*) 88, 96, 98, 120, 158
crested caracara (*Polyborus plancus*) 116
cuajilote *(Pseudobombax palmeri)* 132
DDT 46, 50, 58, 60, 158
desert 44, 69, 74, 90, 158
deciduous forest 48
desert cotton (*Gossypium thurberi*) 102
desert ironwood tree (*Olneya tesota*) 48, 96, 136
desert night-blooming cereus (*Peniocereus greggii*) 98, 114
desert pupfish (*Cyprinodon macularius*) 32
desert scrub 12, 14, 48, 56, 66, 80, 98, 100, 102, 108, 116, 122

162

desert tortoise (*Gopherus agassizii*) 8-10
desert spoon (*Dasylirion wheeleri*) 92
development,
    land 6, 14, 22, 54, 86, 88, 100
    urban 62, 69, 108
    residential 10, 48, 130
    commercial 130
    agricultural 10, 69, 114
drought 10, 28, 38, 44, 56, 58, 66, 84, 88, 96, 122
dry tropical forest (aka, tropical dry forest, tropical deciduous forest) 132, 136, 161
dune evening primrose (*Oenothera deltoides*) 120
dung beetles 68
eastern yellow-billed cuckoo (*Coccyzus americanus americanus*) 70
Echinocereus sciurus floresii 94
Echinocereus scopulorum 94
el lobo 82
el tigrillo 86
elegant tern (*Sterna elegans*) 130
elegant trogon (*Trogon elegans*) 116
elephant trees (*Bursera* spp.) 132
Endangered Species Act (ESA) 32, 50, 70, 84, 156
Endangered Species List 18, 20, 22, 30, 46, 48, 50, 52, 54, 56, 69, 70, 74, 82, 86, 92, 114
ferrets 72, 74
ferruginous hawk (*Buteo regalis*) 74, 118
fire, natural 26, 56, 116
    unnatural or catastrophic 10, 40, 48, 84, 96, 104, 108, 122
fire suppression 84
firewood 80
fish hawks 60
fountaingrass (*Pennisetum setaceum*) 122
frogs 18, 24, 26, 28, 76, 86, 118, 124
Fort Huachuca 126
fur trade 76, 78, 86
gazelle (*Gazella* spp.) 88
giant brown sea cucumber (*Parastichopus fuscus*) 130
giant sand dollar (*Encope micropora*) 42
giant spotted whiptail (*Aspidoscelis burti stictogrammus*) 12

Gila chub (*Gila intermedia*) 32, 36, 122
Gila monster (*Heloderma suspectum*) 10, 14, 16
Gila Mountains 100
Gila National Forest 82
Gila River 36, 124
Gila topminnow (*Poeciliopsis occidentalis sonoriensis*) 36, 122
Gila trout (*Oncorhynchus gilae*) 30
gill nets 130
Goodding willow (*Salix gooddingii*) 124
Gran Desierto de Altar 120
Grand Canyon 52, 120
grassland (*see also* semi-desert grassland) 24, 36, 38, 56, 58, 69, 80, 82, 88, 100, 116
gray fox (*Urocyon cinereoargenteus*) 84
gray hawk (*Asturina nitida*) 118, 124
gray wolf (*Canis lupus*) 82, 118, 136
grazing 24, 30, 44, 54, 56, 94, 98, 116, 132
great horned owl (*Bubo virginianus*) 68, 84, 122
green kingfisher (*Chloroceryle americana*) 124
grizzly bear (*Ursus arctos horribilis*) 118
groundwater pumping 32, 44, 126
guayacan tree (*Guaiacum coulteri*) 132
Gulf chiton (*Chiton virgulatus*) 42
Gulf giant keyhole sand dollar (*Encope grandis*) 42
Gulf of California (aka, Sea of Cortez) 20, 22, 42, 120, 128-130, 136, 137
Gulf pitar (*Pitar vulneratus*) 42
Gunnison prairie dog (*Cynomys gunnisoni*) 74
habitat conversion 14, 46, 94, 96, 106, 114
hackberry (*Celtis* spp.) 62, 102
hawk moths 98, 102
hawksbill sea turtle (*Eretmochelys imbricata*) 22
hedgehogs (*Echinocereus* spp.) 92, 94, 114
History of the U. S. Borderlands 120
horn shark (*Heterodontus francisci*) 128
house mouse (*Mus musculus*) 80
Huachuca giant skipper (*Agathymus evansi*) 40
Huachuca Mountains 18, 40, 66, 124
hummingbirds 66, 92, 94, 116, 118, 136
humpback chub (*Gila cypha*) 34
illegal collection 14, 92, 108
indigo snake (*Drymarchon corais*) 132

invertebrates, aquatic 42
Isla Rasa 130
island gigantism 20
IUCN 156
jaguar (*Panthera onca*) 26, 76, 116, 132
Joseph Banks 138
kapok tree (*Ceiba pentandra*) 132
Kearny sumac (*Rhus kearneyi kearneyi*) 100
Kearny's bluestar (*Amsonia kearneyana*) 102, 116
kit fox (*Vulpes macrotis*) 120
largemouth bass (*Micropterus salmoides*) 32, 38
lazuli bunting (*Passerina amoena*) 116
least Bell's vireo (*Vireo bellii pusillus*) 54
least tern (*Sternula antillarum*) 116
leatherback sea turtle (*Dermochelys coriacea*) 22
Lehmann lovegrass (*Eragrostis lehmanniana*) 116
leopard frogs (*Lithobates pipiens* complex) 18, 26, 28, 118
lesser long-nosed bat (*Leptonycteris curasoae*) 106, 137
lilac-crowned parrot (*Amazona finschi*) 132
Lithobates spp. 18, 26, 28
loach minnow (*Tiaroga cobitis*) 36, 118
loggerhead sea turtle (*Caretta caretta*) 22
long lines, in fishing 22, 130
Louis Agassiz 1
lowland leopard frog (*Lithobates yavapaiensis*) 28, 124
macaws 76, 132
Madrean evergreen woodland 122
Mammillaria saboae goldii 112
Mammillaria saboae haudeana 112
mangrove 6, 50, 76, 128
margay (*Leopardus wiedii*) 78, 132
masked bobwhite (*Colinus virginianus ridgwayi*) 56, 116
mehuele 106
Merriam's mouse (*Peromyscus merriami*) 80
mesquite (*Prosopis* spp.) 48, 56, 58, 62, 80, 98, 102, 116
mesquite mouse (*Peromyscus merriami*) 80
Mexican beaded lizard (*Heloderma horridum*) 16, 132
Mexican blue oak (*Quercus oblongifolia*) 102

163

Mexican gray wolf *(Canis lupus baileyi)* 82, 136
Mexican spotted owl *(Strix occidentalis lucida)* 124
Mexican stoneroller *(Campostoma ornatum)* 38
mining 8, 26, 92, 104, 108, 116, 118, 120
monkeyflowers *(Mimulus* spp.*)* 118
Montezuma bald cypress (aka, Mexican bald cypress, *ahuehuete,* or *sabino) (Taxodium mucronatum)* 132
moon snail *(Polinices recluzianus)* 42
mosquitofish *(Gambusia affinis)* 24, 30, 32, 38, 122, 124
motmots 132
mountain lion *(Puma concolor)* 18, 24, 30, 86, 88, 116, 118, 124
mountain mahogany *(Cercocarpus montanus)* 92
mountain plover *(Charadrius montanus)* 74
Mt. Graham International Observatory 84
Mt. Graham red squirrel *(Tamiasciurus hudsonicus grahamensi)* 84
mule deer *(Odocoileus hemionus)* 124
murex 42
mussels, freshwater 42
Neotropical migrant 70
Nichol's Turk's head cactus *(Echinocactus horizonthalonius* var. *nicholii)* 104, 137
nine-banded armadillo *(Dasypus novemcinctus)* 132
nonnative species 20, 24, 30, 54
    bullfrogs 38
    cowbird 44, 54
    fish 24, 34, 36, 38, 118
    grasses 10, 48, 108
    polyp 122
    salamander 24
    trees 118
northern aplomado falcon *(Falco femoralis)* 58
northern beardless-tyrannulet *(Camptostoma imberbe)* 124
northern bobwhite *(Colinus virginianus)* 56
northern goshawk *(Accipiter gentilis)* 84
northern leopard frog *(Lithobates pipiens)* 28
ocelot *(Leopardus pardalis sonoriensis)* 76, 78, 86, 124, 136
off-road vehicles 10, 92, 96, 104, 108

organ pipe cactus *(Stenocereus thurberi)* 106
Organ Pipe Cactus National Monument 32, 106
organo marismeña 106
osprey *(Pandion haliaetus)* 46, 60
overgrazing 36, 38, 40, 56, 58, 62, 108, 116
owls 48, 56, 68-69, 74, 84, 116, 118, 122, 124
oysters 42
Pacific lion's paw *(Nodipecten subnodosus)* 42
Pacific olive ridley sea turtle *(Lepidochelys olivacea)* 22
palo fierro 96
palo verdes *(Parkinsonia* spp.*)* 88, 98, 122
Panamic pearl oyster *(Pteria sterna)* 42
Peirson's milk-vetch *(Astragalus magdalenae* var. *peirsonii)* 120
pesticides 32, 50, 58, 60, 69, 90, 98
Pima County 80, 108
Pima County Sonoran Desert Conservation Plan 108, 136
Pima pineapple cactus *(Coryphantha robustispina)* 108
Pinacate and Gran Desierto de Altar Biosphere Reserve 120
Pinaleño Mountains 84
pink murex *(Chicoreus regius)* 42
pink sand verbena *(Abronia umbellata)* 120
pink-trumpet tree *(Tabebuia impetiginosa)* 132
pitars 42
pitaya dulce 106
plains leopard frog *(Lithobates blairi)* 28
poaching 20, 50, 52, 78, 88
point-leaf manzanita *(Arctostaphylos pungens)* 92
poison ivy *(Toxicodendron radicans,* aka *Rhus radicans)* 100
porpoise 128, 130
prairie dogs 58, 68-69, 72, 84, 118
Priscilla and Michael Baldwin Foundation *iv*, 138
pronghorn *(Antilocapra americana)* 82, 88, 116
purple dye snail *(Plicopurpura patula)* 42
queen butterfly *(Danaus gilippus)* 118
queen of the night *(reina de la noche)* 98
Quitobaquito pupfish *(Cyprinodon eremus)* 32
raccoon *(Procyon lotor)* 54, 122

raincrow 70
Ramsey Canyon 18
Ramsey Canyon leopard frog *(Lithobates chiricahuensis)* 18, 28
Rana subaquavocalis 18
razorback sucker *(Xyrauchen texanus)* 34
red brome *(Bromus rubens)* 118, 122
red shiner *(Cyprinella lutrensis)* 34, 36, 38
red-tailed hawk *(Buteo jamaicensis)* 84, 122
regal ringneck snake *(Diadophis punctatus regalis)* 118
reina de la noche (queen of the night) 98
reintroduction efforts 18, 26, 28, 36, 38, 52, 58, 64, 72, 82, 88, 102, 116, 126, 160
relict leopard frog *(Lithobates onca)* 28
Rhynchopsitta pachyrhyncha 64
ringtail *(Bassariscus astutus)* 18, 64, 122
Río Cuchujaqui 132
Río Mayo 86
Río Sonoyta 32
Río Yaqui 38, 76, 94
riparian
    forest 48, 66, 70, 159
    corridor 12, 66, 70, 80, 124
    area 32
    vegetation 54, 116
    habitat 66, 70
riparian obligate 44
rock fig *(Ficus petiolaris)* 132
rufous-winged sparrow *(Aimophila carpalis)* 62, 116
Russian thistle or tumbleweed *(Salsola kali)* 118
Sabino Canyon 122
Sabo's pincushion cactus *(Mammillaria saboae)* 112
sacaton *(Sporobolus wrightii)* 38, 62, 124
saguaro *(Carnegiea gigantea)* 48, 106, 118, 122, 137
salt cedar *(Tamarix* spp.*)* 118
San Bernardino Valley 38
San Esteban chuckwalla *(Sauromalus varius)* 20, 137
San Esteban Island 20
San Pedro Riparian National Conservation Area 44, 126

San Pedro River 44, 86, 118, 124-26
San Rafael Valley 18, 24, 58
sand dollars 42
sand food *(Pholisma sonorae)* 120
Santa Catalina Mountains 122
Santinada clam *(Flabellipecten sericeus)* 42
saramatraca 98
sardines 50, 128
Scheer's strong-spined cory cactus *(Coryphantha robustispina)* 108
Scudder, Samuel 1
Sea of Cortez 6, 22, 38, 42, 128-30, 137
sea turtles 22, 128, 130
    leatherback 22
    Pacific olive ridley 22
    loggerhead 22
    hawksbill 22
    black 22
SEMARNAT 157
semi-desert grassland 14, 48, 58, 74, 90, 92, 94, 102, 108, 116, 122, 126
Seri People (Comca'ac) 20, 106
sharks 128, 130
sharp-shinned hawk *(Accipiter striatus)* 84
shovel-nosed sand snake *(Chionactis occipitalis)* 120
Sierra El Viejo 104
Sierra Madre Occidental 26, 64, 112, 160
Sierra San Pedro Martir 52
Sierra Vista 126
Sinaloan white-tailed deer *(Odocoileus virginianus sinaloae)* 132
skippers 40
slate pencil urchin *(Eucidaris thouarsii)* 42
slender climbing cactus *(Echinocereus leucanthus)* 114
snails 42, 122
Sonoran Desert fringe-toed lizard *(Uma notata)* 120
Sonoran Desert scrub 80, 108, 128
Sonoran pronghorn *(Antilocarpa americana sonoriensis)* 88
Sonoran tiger salamander *(Ambystoma mavortium stebbensi)* 24

southwestern willow flycatchers *(Empidonax traillii extimus)* 118
spectacle pod *(Dimorphocarpa pinnatifida)* 120
spikedace *(Meda fulgida)* 36, 118
spiny pitar *(Pitar lupanaria)* 42
spotted bat *(Euderma maculatum)* 90
spotted owl *(Strix occidentalis)* 84
squawbush *(Rhus trilobata)* 92
stingrays 130
stinkbug *(Chlorchroa ligata)* 102
sugar sumac *(Rhus ovata)* 100
sunfishes 26, 34, 36
swift fox *(Vulpes velox)* 74
sycamore *(Platanus wrightii)* 12, 66, 118, 122
sylvatic plague 74
Tarahumara frog *(Lithobates tarahumarae)* 26, 28
tent olive *(Oliva porphyria)* 42
tepeguaje *(Lysiloma watsonii)* 132
terns 116, 128
The Nature Conservancy 18, 118
thick-billed parrot 64, 136
thornscrub 8, 14, 16, 26, 48, 62, 66, 76, 78, 86, 96, 106, 114, 136, 161
tiger salamanders *(Ambystoma mavortium)* 24
tilapia *(tilapia* spp.) 32
Tinajas Altas 100
totoaba *(Totoaba macdonaldi)* 130
tower shell *(Turritella gonostoma)* 42
towhees 44
tree morning glory *(Ipomoea arborescens)* 132
tropical deciduous forest (aka dry tropical forest) 8, 26, 76, 106, 132, 136, 161
trout 30, 34, 36
U.S. Fish and Wildlife Service 48, 116, 156
U.S. Forest Service 12, 40, 116, 157
urchins (sea urchins) 42
vaquita *(Phoecina sinus)* 130
velvet mesquite *(Prosopis velutina)* 102
venomous lizards 14, 16
Verde River 46, 64
vermilion flycatcher *(Pyrocephalus rubinus)* 116
violet-crowned hummingbird *(Amazilia violiceps)* 66, 116

water diversions 32, 34, 44, 88, 116
Waterman Mountains 104
western burrowing owl *(Athene cunicularia hypugaea)* 68-69
western mosquitofish *(Gambusia affinis)* 36, 38
western pipistrelle bat *(Pipistrellus hesperus)* 122
western screech owl *(Megascops kennicottii)* 118
western scrub-jay *(Aphelocoma californica)* 54
western yellow-billed cuckoo *(Coccyzus americanus occidentalis)* 70
white-tailed deer *(Odocoileus virginianus)* 122, 124, 132
Wilcoxia albiflora 114
wolfberry *(Lycium* spp.) 96
woundfin *(Plagopterus argentissimus)* 34
Yaqui catfish *(Ictalurus pricei)* 38
Yaqui chub *(Gila purpurea)* 38
Yaqui sucker *(Catostomus bernardini)* 38
Yaqui topminnow *(Poeciliopsis occidentalis sonoriensis)* 38
yellow bullhead *(Ameiurus natalis)* 124
zauschneria *(Epilobium canum)* 118

Author's Acknowledgments

Just as the character of every individual is shaped by countless influences, from the family and natural environment to the local and international communities, so it is that every publication is the product of many influences and contributions—not only the immediate professional team (artists, contributing essayists, editors, proofreaders, designers, printers) and various shades of volunteer contributors (donors, reviewers, counselors, resource providers, fact-checkers, photographers)—but also supportive family members, inspirational authors, mentors, and friends. In that extended realm, I would like to tender my most heartfelt thanks to Kasey Anderson, who cleared the way at home for me to focus on this project (and countless others).

Of those in the immediate sphere of this publication, I would like to thank the following luminaries. I am most grateful to Priscilla and Michael Baldwin for their boundless inspiration and generosity—for envisioning the Vanishing Circles exhibit, for commissioning the artwork, and shepparding the production of this catalog. In the development of the text, I am deeply grateful to the biologists and ecologists—leaders in their fields already overburdened with tasks—who generously contributed their time and expertise to review the natural-history accounts of the species and landscapes, including: Scott Bonar, Jim Brock, Rick Brusca, Mark Dimmitt, Lloyd Finley, Craig Ivanyi, James L. Jarchow, John Koprowski, Karen Krebbs, Michael Nachman, Stéphane Poulin, John Rinne, Jim Rorabaugh, Cecil Schwalbe, Jeff Seminoff, Dale Turner, and Charles van Riper. I am also enormously grateful to old friends and new acquaintances, also authorities in their fields, who kindly responded to miscellaneous inquiries along the way, including: David Brown, Melanie Culver, Taylor Edwards, Richard Felger, Wendy Hodgson, David Lazaroff, Sue Rutman, and Brian Wakefield, as well as Gene Joseph, who provided counsel and a plethora of cactus references, and Kristen Johnson who lent a critical eye. My sincere gratitude and awe go to Rhonda Spencer, photographer extraordinaire who contributed many hours capturing digital images at the Desert Museum's Art Institute, and to Kim Duffek, whose elegant black-and-white illustrations grace several narratives. I am, of course, deeply grateful to all the men and women who created the fine art for the exhibition and who worked patiently with us to provide both the personal and bureaucratic information we needed. My thanks also extend to some venerable institutions. I would have been at a loss without the friendly staff and abundant references at the University of Arizona Library. I happily acknowledge NatureServe Explorer and the other renowned educational and conservation organizations that compile and post up-to-date information online. I am much indebted to Jim VanderVorste, who provided sound counsel during the design process, and to Susan Fisher, Director of the Arizona-Sonora Desert Museum's Art Institute, who has been a great resource and pillar of support all along. Finally, I am infinitely grateful for the creative vision, guidance, and astute editing of Rick Brusca, Director of the ASDM Press, who has been instrumental in this publication. Throughout the writing and design processes, his confidence, encouragement, patience, and good humor was invaluable.

Linda M. Brewer
October 2010

LINDA M. BREWER is a freelance writer, editor, and graphic designer based in Tucson, Arizona. For two decades, she has worked almost exclusively for environmental and conservation-focused nonprofit organizations, including The Nature Conservancy, Environmental Education Exchange, Arizona-Sonora Desert Museum, and Tucson Botanical Gardens. She has also worked with *American West Magazine*, the University of Arizona Press, and the Tucson Museum of Art, where she served as associate editor of the *Arizona Artist*, a publication funded by the Arizona Commission on the Arts. She has served on the board of the Arizona Native Plant Society and is a contributing author and designer for its popular native-plant brochures.

Ms. Brewer has written for, edited, or designed a spectrum of publications—from gardening guides to children's books and natural-history texts, including *The Arizona Rare Plant Field Guide* and *Land of Black Volcanoes and White Sands—The Pinacate and Gran Desierto de Altar Biosphere Reserve*. She has been editor of the Arizona-Sonora Desert Museum's *Sonorensis* magazine since 2005. In 2007, she was honored with the University of Arizona's Lois Nelson Award for nonfiction writing. Ms. Brewer has also won two coveted IPPYs (Independent Book Publisher's Medal) for Multicultural Books: *The Little Saguaro*, 2008 (for design); and *Katie, of the Sonoran Desert*, 2010 (for text). She has hiked many wonder-filled landscapes in the Sonoran Desert Region—from the thorny hills of the Baja California peninsula to the low deserts, riparian corridors, canyons, and sky islands of Arizona.